The Hispanic Deaf

Issues and Challenges for Bilingual Special Education

Edited by Gilbert L. Delgado

Gallaudet College Press
Washington, D.C.

Gallaudet College Press, Washington, DC 20002
Published 1984
Printed in the United States of America

Library of Congress Cataloging in Publication Data

Main entry under title:

The Hispanic deaf.

 Includes bibliographies and index.
 1. Deaf—Education—United States—Addresses, essays,
lectures.   2. Education, Bilingual—United States—
Addresses, essays, lectures.   3. Hispanic American
children—Education—Addresses, essays, lectures.
I. Delgado, Gilbert L., 1928–   .   II. Blackwell, Peter M.
HV2430.H57   1984   371.91′2′0896873   84-8130
ISBN 0-913580-88-0
Gallaudet College is an equal opportunity employer/educational institution. Programs and services offered by Gallaudet College receive
substantial financial support from the U.S. Department of Education.

Contributors

Peter M. Blackwell
Principal
Rhode Island School for the Deaf
Corliss Park
Providence, RI 02908

Craig Carlisle Dean
26 Bruce Road
Bangor, ME 04401

Gilbert L. Delgado, Ph.D.
Dean
The Graduate School
Gallaudet College
Washington, DC 20002

Joan Good Erickson, Ph.D.
Assistant Professor
Department of Speech &
  Hearing Science
University of Illinois
901 South Sixth Street
Champaign, IL 61820

Richard A. Figueroa, Ph.D.
Associate Professor
Department of Education
University of California
Davis, CA 95616

Joseph E. Fischgrund
(Former Director, Projecto Opor-
  tunidad, Rhode Island School for
  the Deaf)
Director of Academic Affairs
Governor Baxter School for
  the Deaf
P.O. Box 799
Portland, ME 04104

June Grant, Ph.D.
Professor & Director of Special
  Education
Department of Education
Trinity University
715 Stadium Drive
San Antonio, TX 78284

Harriet G. Kopp, Ph.D.
Professor of Communicative
  Disorders &
Acting Dean, College of Human
  Services
San Diego State University
San Diego, CA 92182

Alan Lerman, Ph.D.
Director
Training, Research, & Educational
  Evaluation Division
The Lexington Center, Inc.
30th Avenue & 75th Street
Jackson Heights, NY 11370

Barbara Luetke-Stahlman, Ph.D.
Assistant Professor &
Director, Hearing Impairment
  Program
Department of Counseling &
  Special Education
University of Nebraska at Omaha
Omaha, NE 68182

Donald F. Moores, Ph.D.
Director
Center for Studies in Education
  and Human Development
Gallaudet College
Washington, DC 20002

Julia Maestas y Moores, Ph.D.
Consultant
Washington, D.C.

Nadeen T. Ruiz
Ph.D. Candidate
School of Education
Stanford University
Stanford, CA 94305

Walter G. Secada
Trainer
Bilingual Education Service
   Center
Northwest Educational
   Cooperative
500 South Dwyer Avenue
Arlington Heights, IL 60005

Carmiña Vilá
Assistant Director
Latino In-Service Training &
   Orientation (LISTO) Project
Lexington School for the Deaf
30th Avenue & 75th Street
Jackson Heights, NY 11370

Frederick F. Weiner, Ph.D.
Associate Professor
Department of Communicative
   Disorders
Pennsylvania State University
University Park, PA 16802

THEREFORE, BE IT RESOLVED, that the Conference of Educational Administrators Serving the Deaf take official note of the presence of the significant numbers of Hispanic children in programs for the deaf and call attention to their unique needs and characteristics by recommending that:

1. Recruitment efforts also concentrate on hiring Hispanic professionally trained individuals;

2. Public and information programs be directed to colleges and universities in order to encourage young Hispanics, and other minorities, to consider careers in deafness;

3. Curriculum emphasize a bicultural approach as a means of developing appreciation and understanding of the contributions of Hispanics to the American way of life;

4. Instructional materials be carefully selected for their authenticity and presentation of Hispanic cultural contribution; and

5. Parents and family members from limited or non-English-speaking homes be provided appropriate interpreter services in order to make the home and the school accessible to each other.

Passed: June 21, 1981

Contents

Acknowledgments

My heartfelt appreciation to each of the contributing authors. They are all pioneers, opening trails in unexplored territory. May they have the satisfaction of seeing a growing body of literature on the topic. More importantly, may their work provide the impetus for improved programs and better education for the Hispanic deaf.

Introduction

This book is a response to a present human ecology. For more than two decades, some major demographic changes have been taking place in the U.S. One of the more dramatic changes has been the steady, continuing growth in the number of people from non-English-speaking backgrounds. This is particularly true of the Hispanic* community in this country. Due to a number of factors, discussed in more detail in this book, forecasters believe that Hispanics will be the largest minority group in the U.S. by 1985 or not later than 1990.

These developments have important ramifications for both general education and special education. In terms of general education, the developments have been addressed to some extent through various pieces of legislation, most importantly the Bilingual* Education Act (PL 95-561). The present attitude in the U.S. Department of Education, however, seems to be "let them (Hispanics) find their own level," as if assimilation or the melting pot will take care of everything.

Since its inception, special education has involved disproportionately large numbers of minority children. For example, a recent survey in Prince George's County (Maryland) indicated that 60 percent of its exceptional children were Black. Among exceptional children nationally, Hispanic children constitute the second largest minority group.

These facts clearly require some new awakenings and adjustments in special education. This includes new programming that truly meets the needs of minority, including bilingual/bicultural, students. For Hispanic deaf children in particular, the problem is

---

*Throughout this book we have tried to be consistent in our particular usage of the words *Hispanic* and *bilingual*. *Hispanic* refers to Spanish-surnamed people and their culture, etc. *Bilingual* means regular exposure to, but not necessarily fluency in, two nonmanual languages. By excluding manual languages, this definition of *bilingual* is extremely narrow (one could even say prejudicial). It is used herein only to conform with popular usage (as in the Bilingual Education Act).

that special education has been slow in responding to their fast increasing numbers and needs. The Council for Exceptional Children (CEC) is attempting to address this problem. The CEC has considered it an issue and—through a series of national, topical conferences on the bilingual, special education child—has tried to mesh the well-developed expertise of bilingual/ bicultural education with that of special education. The basis for this collaboration, unfortunately delayed, is that both professions deal with special and often common needs.

The federal picture is much more obscure. Headstart focused on the minority child from lower socioeconomic levels. The majority of these children were Black. The Bilingual Education Act concentrated on children from non-native-language homes, the majority of whom were Hispanic. The Education for All Handicapped Children Act (PL 94-142) focused on children with particular disabilities or combinations thereof. Thus, the lines were drawn. Although some children did filter in and out of this variegated arrangement, administrators of these programs felt compelled to stay within the parameters of their legislation, often literally defined. The result was a good deal of buck-passing and ineffectiveness. Meanwhile, minority children continued to fill special education classrooms.

The number of hearing-impaired children from non-native-language homes is on the rise. With a sense of deja vu, we are also seeing disproportionately large numbers of these children categorized as multihandicapped hearing impaired. In the 1950s educators of the hearing impaired were caught on the horns of a dilemma when they had to deal with cerebral palsy and other motor handicaps along with hearing loss. With the advent of more sophisticated diagnostic tools during the 1960s, the profession realized that it was dealing with a growing population of multihandicapped hearing-impaired children.

Today the bilingual deaf child is in the batter's circle, but the pitchers are sitting in the bull pen and nobody in the stands seems to know what's going on. There appears to be little awareness that a problem exists, let alone programmatic considerations to address the issue.

The epigraph on page v quotes the conclusion of a resolution approved by the Conference of Educational Administrators Serving the Deaf (CEASD) at its 53rd Annual Meeting in Rochester, New York. The CEASD recommendations were a start in the right direction.

This book is another start—the first attempt to compile the work of colleagues who are sensitive to the problem and clearly do not see it going away. The editor hopes that this book will stimulate interest in the area and produce meaningful research, training, and materials.

GILBERT L. DELGADO

Overview

1

Hispanic Deaf Children: A Bilingual and Special Education Challenge

Joan Good Erickson

Individuals who are different from the mainstream by virtue of their racial/ethnic identity *or* handicapping condition have been ignored, oppressed, pitied, ridiculed, or the objects of myriad other pejorative attitudes. Prejudice toward differences and disorders has interfered with the development of appropriate educational policies and procedures. Only in the past two decades have professionals, prompted by litigation and legislation, focused on the educational needs of minority children, shown a renewed interest in bilingual education, and sought to increase appropriate services for children classified as handicapped. More recently, professionals have begun to recognize the unique needs of the bilingual exceptional child. Children with mental, physical, or sensory deficits who are also members of a minority racial/ethnic group in the United States suffer more than one handicap. They are different among the different, a minority within a minority.

The number of people in the U.S. from non-English-language backgrounds was 30 million in 1980 and projected to increase to nearly 40 million by the year 2000 (NACBE, 1981). More than one-third of the language-minority population and 60 percent of language-minority school children, according to estimates, are from Spanish-speaking backgrounds. Conservative incidence figures on handicapping conditions suggest at least 10 percent of any population would be identified as in need of special educational procedures. The incidence of hearing impairments in populations of Hispanic children is less easy to establish. For example, it varies according to demographics, may not include information as to the home language, and is complicated by health, nutrition, and other factors associated with low-income populations.

Severe or profound hearing impairment, although a low-incidence handicap, is a significant sensory disability because of its devastating effect on communication. Thus, children who are both deaf and Hispanic present an educational challenge: in addition to their sensory handicap, which affects speech and language learning and thus academic achievement, their cultural and linguistic differences also must be considered in educational planning. Solutions are complicated by the dearth of research, personnel, and appropriate evaluation and therapeutic procedures designed to serve this population.

This chapter will provide a brief background of the history, litigation, and legislation in bilingual and special education; an overview of recent trends in education of the bilingual exceptional child; and a discussion of the issues regarding minority hearing-impaired children. The purpose of this historical, legal, and educational overview is to introduce the reader to the focus of the text: the education of the Hispanic deaf child in this country.

Development of Bilingual Education

Bilingualism and bilingual education exist worldwide. Indeed, few nations are monolingual; many are multilingual. Bilingual schools have existed in this country since the 1800s, particularly in regions where there are strong ethnic and religious commitments. Discrimination against immigrants and ethnic minorities, especially during World Wars I and II, diminished the opportunities for bilingual education and stressed the acquisition of English (U.S. Commission on Civil Rights, 1975). Inherent in the attitude toward bilingual education is the acceptance or rejection of the ideology of cultural pluralism: the melting pot versus the salad bowl view of being U.S. citizens. Although it has been recognized for many decades that language-minority children educated in English-speaking schools are frequently doomed to academic failure, only recently has there been an aggressive movement to address the needs of non-English-proficient (NEP) children. Bilingual education, therefore, is not a new phenomenon in the United States. Depending on the social, political, and educational climate regarding minority populations, it has received various levels of interest, approval, or support.

The civil rights movement of the 1960s provided the basis for the current focus on bilingual education. Development of social and educational services was prompted by the Civil Rights Act of 1964, which stipulated that no person shall be discriminated against by virtue of race, color, or national origin in any service program receiving federal assistance. Further litigation and judicial action validated the right of language-minority individuals to receive services specific to their needs.

The Bilingual Education Act of 1968 further defined the needs of language-minority children and designated them as a special population in regard to education. This act provided for demonstration programs that would develop bilingual instructional models, curriculum materials, and teacher training programs. Just as litigation a decade earlier *(Brown v. Topeka Board of Education)* established the importance of *equal education* for minorities, the Bilingual Education Act developed further the concept of *equality of educational opportunity.* Further clarification came from the U.S. Department of Health, Education, and Welfare in 1970 with the directive often referred to as the May Memorandum. This policy statement required schools to meet the needs of language-minority children or suffer the loss of funding.

The 1974 Supreme Court decision in *Lau v. Nichols* was heralded for its extensive impact on the education of language-minority children. This class action suit, filed on behalf of 1,800 Chinese-speaking children in San Francisco, claimed that students were denied meaningful instruction if they could not, due to lack of English skills, effectively participate in English-speaking classrooms. Although remedies were not provided, the decision indicated that the school district had violated the civil rights of this group of students and recommended that special language programming be provided. The *Lau* decision did not mandate bilingual education, but it provided the impetus for exploring educational alternatives.

These educational alternatives have varied according to philosophy, goals, and methodology, depending on state and local education agency interpretation and implementation. Approaches also vary depending on the number of language-minority children enrolled in a particular school district. Districts with large minority populations cannot ignore the need for implementing bilingual programs. The fewer the number of minority-language children, the more the emphasis on cultural assimilation and rapid acquisition of English as a second language. Numbers, however, do not ensure the development of bilingual/ bicultural programs; in many localities the political climate supports monolingual and monocultural goals.

No one disputes the importance of an individual having access to mainstream language and culture. The acquisition of the mainstream language in a monolingual nation is necessary in order for individuals to achieve social mobility and economic rewards. The question is not if but how best to achieve this goal and whether or not it should be done at the expense of threatening the cultural and linguistic values of minority individuals. Indeed, the oft-misunderstood goal of bilingual education is that the individual becomes bilingual and biliterate, i.e., proficient in two language systems. This additive rather than subtractive goal is possible when both the first and second languages can be developed to their maximums. Although maintenance of a first language and culture may be viewed by some as a threat to the acquisition of the mainstream language and culture, this notion is unfounded. Bilingualism, particularly when the languages have equal status, enhances rather than diminishes cognitive and educational achievement (Lambert, 1979).

Bilingual Program Models

Models for implementing bilingual education are as varied as the ideologies that dictate their development. Programs vary from tacit consent to maintain the culture of the student while providing English as a second language (ESL) instruction to well-developed curricula providing bilingual learning experiences within a multicultural atmosphere. In bilingual education classrooms, instruction may be provided by a bilingual teacher or, at the minimum, a bilingual aide. The ESL instruction is usually provided on a tutorial basis by a specialist in this area. In some school districts where there are few NEP children (usually interpreted as fewer than 20 children in the same language group), instruction may be provided by the only school personnel trained in language acquisition, the speech/language pathologists. Theoretically, individualized or small-group instruction in English will assist the child in handling the academic challenges of classroom instruction.

There are several models for implementing bilingual programs, all based on various philosophies of language and of cultural maintenance versus assimilation (Trueba, 1979). A frequent approach to bilingual education is the transitional model. For children who enter the educational system with limited English skills, the school district provides a program that allows the child to be instructed in the primary language, provides ESL instruction, and eventually moves the child into an all-English mode of instruction by the second or third grade. Transitional programs vary as to the emphasis placed on first-language development and maintenance. Less frequently available are maintenance models in which ongoing instruction is provided in both languages in a multicultural setting. Maintenance programs stress the development of bilingualism and biliteracy throughout the child's academic career or, at the minimum, through the elementary grades.

Bilingual programs also vary as to how and when the two languages are used for instruction. Some programs designate specific days, half-days, areas of the room, or the teacher/teacher aide for focus on instruction in a particular language. Programs also vary in their emphasis on the development of reading and writing skills versus the development of social communication skills.

The development of sophisticated language skills in both languages must be achieved in order to enhance academic development. Two salient points regarding language proficiency in bilingual education discussed by Cummins (1981) are that (1) it takes significantly less time to develop context-embedded (social) than context-reduced (academic) communicative proficiency; and (2) experiences with either of two languages can promote the proficiency that underlies the development of academic skills in both. In spite of research that supports the goals and rewards of bilingual education (Troike, 1978), local attitudes toward cultural pluralism will eventually dictate program philosophy and implementation. These attitudes—and related variations in financial support for bilingual education programs—may be the basis for program success or failure.

Development of Special Education

History is replete with examples of misunderstanding the learning needs and potential of handicapped individuals. The mentally retarded and mentally ill were shunted away to institutions; only in the past several decades have they been recognized as deserving educational and social opportunity to achieve their fullest in a least restrictive environment. Although deaf people were among the first handicapped individuals to receive special education, they have been misdiagnosed as retarded and misunderstood as to their linguistic, social, and vocational needs. The leadership exhibited by deaf education, however, has been a model for the development of special education programs, such as self-contained classrooms, for other disability groups.

Special education in the 1970s was affected by two federal directives, one related to educational funding and one to the civil rights of handicapped individuals. Public Law 94-142 and Section 504 of the Rehabilitation Act of 1973 affected both educational policy and the civil rights of handicapped people. These federal directives and subsequent litigation had a far-reaching effect on the development of services for children with special needs. These acts also provided educators with directives for planning individualized programs, delineated the importance of parent involvement, and clarified the rights of the handicapped to have access to mainstream society.

Development of Bilingual Special Education

Psychological and educational assessment procedures for minorities have been questioned increasingly by professionals in the past two decades (Oakland, 1977; Samuda, 1975). Research confirmed the suspicion that minority children were misplaced in special education classrooms (Mercer, 1973). A 1970 landmark case in bilingual special education *(Diana v. California State Board of Education)* specified the need to identify and assess the intellectual ability of children in their native languages. Several other court cases substantiated this finding and encouraged school districts to identify and educate language-minority handicapped children appropriately.

Approaches to assessing the communication skills of bilingual children have moved away from the use of discrete point tests and toward integrative measures (Erickson & Omark, 1981; Oller, 1979). This movement occurred as an attempt to lessen discriminatory testing procedures and more accurately reflect the synergistic and contextual features of language use. The efficacy of these types of assessment procedures with bilingual handicapped children is yet to be established.

Although there is increasing knowledge about the acquisition of languages other than English, little is known regarding language acquisition among bilingual handicapped children. There is also a lack of research on whether a bilingual or monolingual approach to educating the handicapped language-minority child is most effective. Case histories and theoretical conjectures are the primary bases used in support of current approaches (Greenlee, 1981; Omark & Erickson, 1983). There are also numerous questions regarding which educational procedures are most appropriate for handicapped language-minority children. Some of these questions are inherent to special education. Others involve bilingual education, including the literature which deals with sociolinguistic phenomena such as code-mixing and switching and other aspects of language use.

Although there are geographical pockets of interest in the education of minority/handicapped children, there has been a lack of educational aggressiveness in providing appropriate educational programs for this population. The interfacing of bilingual and special education has been a slow process that only recently has received national attention (Bergin, 1980). Complicating the development of these combined fields has been the lack of research and trained personnel. The importance of providing nondiscriminatory assessment and bilingual education for minority/handicapped populations has been validated legally and professionally; the educational solutions, however, are far from clear.

Whether or not bilingualism is the most realistic goal for a child with an intellectual or sensory deficit is open to question. Depending on the potential of the child and the attitudes of the family and the community, how can monolingual or bilingual goals best be achieved? The concepts of equal education and equality of educational opportunity are as salient an issue with this population as with minority-language populations in general. On the one hand, if the minority language is used as the medium for instructing children with sensory barriers, does this have the effect of alienating them from the mainstream? On the other hand, if the mainstream language is chosen for the medium of instruction, what effect does this have on alienating children from their families and cultures? Thus far, local policy rather than empirical evidence has been the basis for selecting the language(s) of instruction with this population.

One might question whether or not the school has the right to impose a goal of learning English on the primary models and caretakers of the handicapped child, the parents. It is also important to evaluate the effect that minimal English-skilled models have on language development of the handicapped child. Furthermore, consideration should be given to the rights of the handicapped child who may be forced to function in a language environment chosen by educators. A basic consideration in bilingual education is that there be agreement between the school administration, the parents, *and* the community in regard to bilingual versus monolingual instruction and transitional versus maintenance models. This same tenet should be applied to education of handicapped language-minority children. Education policy and programming cannot be made in a vacuum.

Education of the exceptional minority child, prompted by legal action and influenced by professional commitment, presents a unique challenge to several fields including special/deaf education, audiology, speech/language pathology, applied linguistics, and bilingual education. Educators of the hearing impaired have shown leadership in the field of special education. Bilingual educators continue to develop and provide appropriate programs for language-minority populations. Professionals in bilingual and special education who recognize the needs of the handicapped bilingual child are now beginning to address the topic of the Hispanic deaf child. The purpose of this text is to explore these issues and challenges.

References

Bergin, V. *Special education needs in bilingual programs.* Washington, D.C.: National Clearinghouse for Bilingual Education, 1980.

Cummins, J. Four misconceptions about language proficiency in bilingual education. *NABE Journal, 5*(3), 1981, 31–45.

Erickson, J.G., & Omark, D.R. *Communication assessment of the bilingual bicultural child: Issues and guidelines.* Baltimore: University Park Press, 1981.

Greenlee, M. Specifying the needs of a "bilingual" developmentally disabled population: Issues and case studies. *NABE Journal, 6*(1), 1981, 55–76.

Lambert, W.E. Language as a factor in intergroup relations. In H. Giles and R. St. Clair (Eds.), *Language and social psychology.* Baltimore: University Park Press, 1979.

Mercer, J.R. *Labeling the mentally retarded.* Berkeley: University of California Press, 1973.

National Advisory Council for Bilingual Education. *The prospects for bilingual education in the nation* (NACBE Fifth Annual Report, 1980–81). Washington, D.C.: Author, 1981.

Oakland, T.M. (Ed.). *Psychological and educational assessment of minority children.* New York: Brunner/Mazel, 1977.

Oller, J.W. *Language tests at school.* London: Longman, 1979.

Omark, D.R., & Erickson, J.G. *The bilingual exceptional child.* San Diego: College-Hill Press, 1983.

Samuda, R.J. *Psychological testing of American minorities: Issues and consequencies.* New York: Harper and Row, 1975.

Troike, R.C. Research evidence for the effectiveness of bilingual education. *NABE Journal, 3,* 1978, 13–24.

Trueba, H.T. Bilingual education models: Types and designs. In H.T. Trueba and C. Barnett-Mizrahi (Eds.), *Bilingual multicultural education and the professional: From theory to practice.* Rowley, Mass.: Newbury House, 1979.

U.S. Commission on Civil Rights. *A better chance to learn: Bilingual bicultural education* (Clearinghouse Publication No. 51). Washington, D.C.: National Clearinghouse for Bilingual Education, 1975.

The Hispanic Deaf Population

2

The Status of Hispanics in Special Education

Julia Maestas y Moores and Donald F. Moores

Historically, contributions by Hispanic individuals to special education have been monumental. Three Hispanic individuals—Pedro Ponce de Leon, Juan Pablo Bonet, and Jacobo Rodriguez Pereira in the sixteenth, seventeenth, and eighteenth century, respectively—generated many of the educational procedures employed today in special education. Scientific observation; a case history approach; individualized instruction; sense training; a developmental approach to language; a kinesthetic, analytic approach to speech and reading; the establishment of programs to educate deaf individuals; the use of fingerspelling and possibly signs; and the first published book on the education of the deaf can all be attributed to these three Hispanic educators (Maestas y Moores, in progress).

In 1981 data were gathered on the employment of Hispanic educators in special education and the provision of special education services to Hispanic students (Maestas, 1981a). The data came from a variety of sources, including the U.S. Bureau of the Census, the National Center for Education Statistics, the Office of Civil Rights, the Office of Special Education and Rehabilitative Services, the Equal Employment Opportunity Commission, and the Gallaudet Center for Assessment and Demographic Studies.

In recent years people have become increasingly aware of the presence and impact of the Hispanic population in the U.S. The 1980 census (Table 1) reported 14,612,303 Hispanics in the 50 states and District of Columbia, an increase of 5,536,753 Hispanics or approximately 61 percent from 1970 to 1980. Additionally, the island of Puerto Rico reported a population of 3,187,570 in 1980. This figure represented an increase of 475,537 over the 1970 census. When the Puerto Rico total was included in the U.S. figure, the grand total was almost 18,000,000 Hispanics.

Caution should be exercised in discussing the growth of the Hispanic population. There were major undercounts of Hispanics in the 1970

Table 1
Hispanic Population in the United States:
States in Rank Order by 1980 Enumeration

State	1970 Census	1980 Census	Change	Percent Change
California	2,369,292	4,543,770	2,174,478	91.8
Texas	1,840,648	2,985,643	1,144,995	62.2
New York	1,351,982	1,659,245	307,263	22.7
Florida	405,036	857,898	452,862	111.7
Illinois	393,204	635,525	242,321	61.6
New Jersey	288,488	491,867	203,379	70.5
New Mexico	308,340	476,089	167,749	54.4
Arizona	264,770	440,915	176,145	66.5
Colorado	225,506	339,300	113,794	50.5
Michigan	151,070	162,388	11,318	7.5
Pennsylvania	108,893	154,004	45,111	41.4
Massachusetts	66,146	141,063	74,917	113.3
Connecticut	65,456	124,499	59,043	90.2
Washington	57,358	119,986	62,628	109.2
Ohio	129,995	119,880	−10,115	−7.8
Louisiana	70,523	99,105	28,582	40.5
Indiana	112,472	87,020	−25,452	−22.6
Virginia	40,222	79,873	39,651	98.6
Hawaii	24,821	71,479	46,658	188.0
Oregon	22,338	65,833	43,495	194.7
Maryland	45,461	64,740	19,279	42.4
Kansas	54,125	63,333	9,208	17.0
Wisconsin	62,875	62,981	106	0.2
Georgia	45,289	61,261	15,972	35.3
Utah	33,911	60,302	26,391	77.8
Oklahoma	51,284	57,413	6,129	12.0
North Carolina	43,414	56,607	13,193	30.4
Nevada	20,505	53,786	33,281	162.3

State	1970 Census	1980 Census	Change	Percent Change
Missouri	60,080	51,667	−8,413	−14.0
Idaho	16,077	36,615	20,538	127.7
Tennessee	49,584	34,081	−15,503	−31.3
Alabama	38,848	33,100	−5,748	−14.8
South Carolina	14,111	33,414	19,303	136.8
Minnesota	37,256	32,124	−5,132	−13.8
Nebraska	20,749	28,020	7,271	35.0
Kentucky	44,749	27,403	−17,346	−38.8
Iowa	21,017	25,536	4,519	21.5
Mississippi	18,815	24,731	5,916	31.4
Wyoming	13,894	24,499	10,605	76.3
Rhode Island	7,589	19,707	12,118	159.7
Arkansas	24,358	17,873	−6,485	−26.6
District of Columbia	15,108	17,652	2,544	16.8
West Virginia	8,780	12,707	3,927	44.7
South Dakota	2,876	10,428	7,552	262.6
Montana	6,344	9,974	3,630	57.2
Delaware	8,477	9,671	1,194	14.1
Alaska	4,598	9,497	4,899	106.5
New Hampshire	2,281	5,587	3,306	144.9
Maine	2,433	5,005	2,572	105.7
North Dakota	2,492	3,903	1,411	56.6
Vermont	1,610	3,304	1,694	105.2
Total	9,075,550	14,612,303	5,536,753	61.0
Puerto Rico	2,712,033	3,187,570	475,537	17.5

Note. From *Age, Sex, Race, & Spanish Origin of the Population by Region, Division, and States, 1980* (United States Department of Commerce News). Washington, D.C.: U.S. Bureau of the Census, Office of Public Information, May 1981.

census that were partially corrected in 1980. According to the census bureau, modifications in the 1980 census, better coverage of the population, improved question design, and an effective public relations campaign by national and community relations groups resulted in a more efficient enumeration of Hispanics in 1980 than in 1970. It is probable, however, that undercounts of Hispanics in the 1980 census were still greater than undercounts of the general population. Therefore, the reported total of 14,642,303 Hispanics in the U.S. may be considered an underenumeration of undetermined size.

Table 1, which presents information on Hispanic population by state, reveals some interesting data. Increases in the Hispanic population from 1970 to 1980 are most noticeable in California, with an increase of 2,000,000; Texas with 1,000,000; Florida with almost 500,000; and New York, Illinois, and New Jersey with increases of 200,000 to 300,000. The Hispanic population grew by more than 50 percent in 8 of the 10 states which had the largest numbers of Hispanics. Among these states the largest percentage increases were in Florida (111 percent), California (91 percent), and New Jersey (70 percent).

In terms of percentage of total state population, New Mexico had the highest proportion of Hispanics (36 percent) followed by Texas (21 percent) and California (19 percent). Another noticeable factor is the geographic diversity of the Hispanic population. Five of the 12 most populous Hispanic states (California, Texas, New Mexico, Arizona, Colorado) are in a southwestern cluster; three (New York, New Jersey, Pennsylvania) are in the Northeast; two (Illinois and Michigan) are in the Midwest; and one (Florida) is in the Southeast.

Examination of Table 1 reveals that the five most populous Hispanic states—California, Texas, New York, Florida, and Illinois—accounted for 4,321,919 of the 5,566,753 national increase of Hispanics between 1970 and 1980. These five states had more than 10,600,000 Hispanics (73 percent of the U.S. Hispanic population) according to the 1980 census. It should be pointed out, however, that many other states had equal or greater proportional growth and that Hispanics constitute a significant presence across the nation. As shown in Table 2 census data, the Hispanic population more than doubled in 14 states from 1970 to 1980. Only one of the most populous states, Florida, was in this category. The states with more than 100 percent increases in their Hispanic population ranged from states in the Northwest (Washington, Oregon, Nevada, Idaho) to the Northeast (Massachusetts, Rhode Island, Vermont, Maine, New Hampshire). The number of Hispanics also doubled in South Carolina, South Dakota, Alaska, and Hawaii.

Table 2
Change in Hispanic Population in the 50 States, 1970 to 1980:
Rank Ordered by Percentage of Change

State	Percent Change	Number Change
South Dakota	262.5	7,552
Oregon	194.7	43,495
Hawaii	188.0	46,658
Nevada	162.3	33,281
Rhode Island	159.7	12,118
New Hampshire	144.9	3,306
South Carolina	136.6	19,303
Idaho	127.2	20,538
Massachusetts	113.3	74,917
Florida	111.7	452,862
Washington	109.2	62,628
Alaska	106.5	4,899
Maine	105.7	2,572
Vermont	105.2	1,694
Virginia	98.6	39,651
California	91.8	2,174,478
Connecticut	90.2	59,043
Utah	77.8	26,391
Wyoming	76.3	10,605
New Jersey	70.5	203,379
Arizona	66.5	176,145
Texas	62.2	1,144,995
Illinois	61.6	242,321
Montana	57.2	3,630
North Dakota	56.6	1,411
New Mexico	54.4	167,749

State	Percent Change	Number Change
Colorado	50.5	113,794
West Virginia	44.7	3,927
Maryland	42.4	19,279
Pennsylvania	41.4	45,111
Louisiana	40.5	28,582
Georgia	35.3	15,972
Nebraska	35.0	7,271
North Carolina	30.4	13,193
New York	22.7	307,263
Iowa	21.5	4,519
Kansas	17.0	9,208
District of Columbia	16.8	2,544
Delaware	14.1	1,194
Oklahoma	12.0	6,129
Michigan	7.5	11,318
Wisconsin	0.2	106
Ohio	−7.8	−10,115
Minnesota	−13.8	−5,132
Missouri	−14.0	−8,413
Alabama	−14.8	−5,748
Indiana	−22.6	−25,452
Arkansas	−26.6	−6,485
Tennessee	−31.3	−15,503
Mississippi	−31.4	−5,916
Kentucky	−38.8	−17,346

Young Age, Old History

The term *Hispanic* encompasses diverse populations with Chicano, Puerto Rican, Cuban, Central American, and South American roots. Although diverse, the various people share a Spanish colonial tradition and culture and the Spanish language.

It is difficult to characterize such a diverse population. However, some general statements can be made. Generally, U.S. Hispanics are younger than the general population. Their average age is approximately 21, 10 years younger than the national average for non-Hispanics. The distribution of Hispanics in various age groups varies, however. Hill (1980) reported that Hispanics account for 4.4 percent of the total population age 16 and above. Contrasted to this is an analysis of 1978 civil rights data (Killelea Associates, 1980) which reported that, of a total elementary and secondary school enrollment of 41,856,257 students, 6.8 percent or 2,825,229 were Hispanic. The Hispanic preschool population is even greater. A census bureau report (1980) reported that almost 10 percent of all students in the U.S. under five years of age were Hispanic in origin.

Hispanic roots in the U.S. are old and deep. The Hispanic presence both in the U.S. and in the Western Hemisphere precedes that of the English-speaking population. Northern New Mexico was settled in 1598 prior to the English landings in Jamestown, Virginia and Plymouth, Massachusetts. St. Augustine, Florida, founded by the Spanish, is the only U.S. city eligible to celebrate its 400th anniversary. Puerto Rico had a Spanish settlement before the year 1500. The extent of the Hispanic presence in the U.S. may be illustrated by the fact that most of the land in the contiguous 48 states was at one time or another part of the Spanish colonial empire, stretching from Florida to California, from Louisiana to Minnesota, and from Minnesota to the Pacific. California and Texas have had an Hispanic presence for more than 200 years and New Mexico for 400 years.

Special Education

Although relatively little information is available on the quality and type of special education services presently provided to Hispanic children, data have been collected and analyzed on the numbers of Hispanic children in special education programs in the United States. The 1978 civil rights survey reported Hispanic enrollment in special education programs (Table 3). At a time when Hispanics represented 7 percent of the total U.S. elementary and secondary school enrollment,

Table 3
Hispanic Participation and Total Enrollment
in Selected Special Education Programs
in the United States, Fall 1978

Category	Total Enrollment	Hispanic Enrollment	Hispanic Percentage of Total Enrollment
Specific Learning Disabilities	962,111	72,620	7.5
Trainable Mentally Retarded	95,083	6,588	6.9
Severely Emotionally Disturbed	135,400	8,315	6.1
Speech Impaired	826,385	49,756	6.0
Educable Mentally Retarded	596,878	27,548	4.6
Total	2,615,857	164,827	6.3
Gifted/ Talented	810,386	41,521	5.1

Note. From *State, Regional, and National Summaries of Data from the 1978 Civil Rights Survey of Elementary and Secondary Schools.* Alexandria, Va.: Killelea Associates, 1980, p. 105.

they constituted 6 percent of the enrollment in programs for the handi-capped and 5 percent of the enrollment in programs for the gifted and talented. Within the five categories of handicapping condition, there appeared to be little variation. As percentages of total enrollment, Hispanics represented nearly 5 percent of the children classified as educable mentally retarded, 6 percent of the speech impaired and the emotionally disturbed, 7 percent of the trainable mentally retarded, and nearly 8 percent of the children with specific learning disabilities. The results in each category are close to what would be expected given Hispanic student representation in elementary and secondary schools in the United States.

Table 4
Enrollment in Programs for the Hearing Impaired, 1978–1979

Ethnic Category	Number	Percent of Total
White	34,193	70.3
Black	8,487	17.4
Hispanic	4,564	9.4
Other	1,424	2.9
Total	48,668	100.0

Note. Data provided the author by the Center for Assessment and Demographic Studies, Gallaudet College, July 1982.

Table 5
Ethnic Background: Teachers of the Hearing Impaired, 1978–1979

Ethnic Category	Number	Percent of Total
White	4,583	93.8
Black	159	3.3
Hispanic	30	0.6
Oriental	47	1.0
American Indian	12	0.2
Other	9	0.2
Not Reported	47	1.0
Total	4,887	100.1

Note. From *Teachers of the Deaf: Descripitive Profiles* by E. Corbett, Jr., and C. Jensema. Washington, D.C.: Gallaudet College Press, 1981, p.13. Copyright 1981 by Gallaudet College. Reprinted by permission. The authors used the term *Spanish-American* for *Hispanic.* Percentages add to more than 100 percent due to rounding.

Other data—of particular interest to readers of this book—show that Hispanics are enrolled in proportionately greater numbers in programs for the deaf, accounting for 9.4 percent of enrollment in 1978–79 (Table 4). The figure is more than one-third higher than would be expected. The reasons for this relatively high enrollment are not clear. What is clear is the large discrepancy between the figures on Hispanic *students* in programs for the deaf and on Hispanic *teachers* of the deaf.

Table 4 shows that whites comprise approximately 70 percent of student enrollment in programs for the deaf, Blacks 17 percent, and Hispanics 9 percent. Table 5 shows sharply contrasting data on the racial/ethnic background of teachers of the deaf in the U.S. If the ethnic background of these teachers paralleled that of their hearing-impaired students, we might expect about 3,420 of the teachers to be white, 830 to be Black, and 440 to be Hispanic. What we find (Table 5) is a total of 30 Hispanic teachers of the deaf, or less than 1 percent of the teachers surveyed.

The Larger Pattern

The small number of Hispanic teachers of the deaf appears to be part of a larger pattern. Various data indicate significantly lower percentages of Hispanic teachers in special education than in education in general. For example, the National Education Association (NEA) reported in 1980 that there were 54,000 Hispanics in a membership of 1,750,000, or slightly more than 3 percent of the total. The Council for Exceptional Children (CEC) had a 1980 membership of 46,976, of whom only 172 or less than 0.4 percent were Hispanic. Only 90 of 14,532 student members of CEC were Hispanics, or 0.6 percent of the total. The CEC had a 10-person executive committee, 72-member board of governors, and 55 federation and branch presidents. There were no Hispanics in any of these groups (Maestas, 1981a).

At the federal level, the Office of Special Education and Rehabilitative Services (OSERS) had a 1980 budget of $2 billion for activities including direct aid to states, supplemental support for local and regional programs, support of preservice and inservice training, grants to centers for a wide range of programmatic research, and funding of demonstration projects in areas such as early childhood special education and programming for severely and profoundly handicapped children. The office has directed considerable resources to monitoring implementation of PL 94-142, the Education for all Handicapped Children Act.

The OSERS has heavily influenced inservice and preservice training, research and demonstration activities, and educational programs by its allocation of funds and monitoring activities. It has a tremendous impact on special education across the nation. Because its support is crucial for any significant advances in the Hispanic population, OSERS should reflect sensitivity toward the needs of Hispanics who are handicapped, gifted and talented, or professionals and professionals in training.

Within this context, the situation is disquieting. In 1981 the U.S. Department of Education (of which OSERS is a part) employed 178 Hispanics in a staff of 5,609, or approximately 3 percent of the total. This figure is consistent with reported figures of NEA membership. According to information provided by the OSERS executive staff and the Equal Employment Office of the Department of Education, OSERS in February 1981 employed four Hispanics, or 0.8 percent of the total staff of 513. Two Hispanics were statisticians employed in Washington, D.C., one was a secretary employed in Texas, and one was a project officer employed in Colorado.

The field of special education, then, appears to be behind general education in the training, recruitment, and utilization of Hispanic professionals. Why is there such a discrepancy? Why is there 3.0 percent Hispanic representation in NEA and only 0.4 percent in CEC? Why is there 3.0 percent Hispanic representation in the Department of Education and only 0.8 percent in OSERS?

The answers, of course, are not clear. Speculation might suggest that special education has had a tradition of paternalism and racism. The greatest example of this was the proliferation in the 1950s, 1960s, and early 1970s of classes for the so-called "educable mentally retarded" (EMR) children. It is no secret that disproportionate numbers of Hispanic children were misdiagnosed as EMR, branded as retarded, and segregated into special classrooms.

Even before the EMR movement, special education had unfortunate relationships with repressive, exclusionary strains in U.S. history. Nearly 100 years ago, A.G. Bell wrote his *Memoir: Upon the Formation of a Deaf Variety of the Human Race,* in which he proposed ways to prevent intermarriage of deaf people so as to prevent the growth of a race of what he referred to as "undesirable" and "defective" people. And in the twentieth century, the influence of the eugenics movement has initiated the study of racial differences in intelligence.

Exclusion and Discrimination

These unpleasant aspects of the history of special education have several ramifications. First, there is evidence that, until recently, special education has had little documented positive influence in the lives of Hispanic individuals. In fact, much of that influence has been negative, ranging from excluding to misdiagnosing Hispanic handicapped students. Second, although there have been improvements, many of the individuals in decision-making roles operate under the legacy of discrimination that historically has bordered on racism. Consciously or unconsciously they may accept some of the stereotypes so harmful to Hispanics. A third factor may be the distrust many Hispanics have toward special education. They know of its past racist policies and its present insensitivity. More often than not special education is perceived as more of a threat than a help.

Thus, special education is faced with a situation potentially dangerous to Hispanic handicapped students. Despite past injustices, there *are* Hispanic children who are learning disabled, retarded, disturbed, deaf, and gifted. They probably exist in much the same proportions as in any other group.

While the practice of inappropriately labeling large numbers of Hispanic children as EMR seems to be alleviated, there continues to be a seriously low number of Hispanic teachers in special education as compared to general education. This must be remedied. Often it has been suggested that only Hispanic teachers can teach Hispanic children or that quotas should be established for teachers. In a pluralistic society it is unrealistic to argue that Black, Hispanic, German, English, or Japanese children, for example, can be taught only by their own kind. Non-Hispanic teachers can and do teach Hispanic children. The problem is that many people do not realize that Hispanic teachers can and should teach non-Hispanic children. Often predominantly Hispanic special education programs are taught and administered entirely by non-Hispanics. Seldom is the reverse true.

The second issue—that of so-called quotas—has been distorted to the extent that it is used to justify the continuation of racist policies. Some special educators have argued that the push to recruit more Hispanic teachers would lower standards. They do not acknowledge that, by excluding Hispanics from special education for so many years, the nation has failed to utilize a significant proportion of its creative potential. This is not to say that all groups should be represented in every field in direct proportion to its percentage in the population. However, when less than 1 percent of the nation's special education teachers are Hispanic, the facts point to a continuing pattern of exclusion and discrimination that must be rectified.

References

Bell, A. G. *Memoir: Upon the formation of a deaf variety of the human race.* Washington, D.C.: A. G. Bell Association for the Deaf, 1969.

Hay, B. 14.6 millones de Hispanos en los Estados Unidos (Segun el censo de 1980). *U.S. Department of Commerce News.* Washington, D.C.: Bureau of the Census, Officina de Informacion Publica, February 27, 1981.

Higher Education Reporting Committee. *Equal Employment Opportunity Commission higher education staff information.* Washington, D.C.: National Education Association, 1979.

Hill, S., & Froomkin, J. *Characteristics of Hispanic postsecondary students.* Washington, D.C.: National Center for Educational Statistics, 1978.

Jensema, C., & Corbett, E. *Teachers of the deaf: Descriptive profiles.* Washington, D.C.: Gallaudet College Press, 1981.

Killelea Associates. *State, regional, and national summaries of data from the 1978 civil rights survey of elementary and secondary schools.* Alexandria, Va.: Author, 1980.

Maestas, J. *The participation of Hispanics in special education.* Paper presented at the Institute for Educational Leadership, George Washington University, March 4, 1981. (a)

Maestas, J. *Analysis of "Hispanic-related" grants.* Unpublished report prepared for the U.S. Office of Education, September 1981. (b)

Maestas, J. *Contributions of Spanish individuals to special education.* In progress.

National Center for Education Statistics. *Fall enrollment in institutions of higher education—1979* (Higher Education General Information Survey). Washington, D.C.: U.S. Bureau of the Census, 1979.

Saintz, P. Numbers of teachers employed in special education across the United States according to the office of Special Education and Rehabilitative Services, Division of Planning and Personnel. Personal communication, December 1980.

Status of teachers and NEA members. Washington, D.C.: National Education Association, September 1980.

U.S. Bureau of the Census. *Persons of Spanish origin in the United States* (Current Population Reports, Series P-20, No. 339, March 1978).Washington, D.C.: U.S. Government Printing Office, 1978.

U.S. Bureau of the Census. *Persons of Spanish origin in the United States* (Current Population Reports, Series P-20, No. 354, March 1979).Washington, D.C.: U.S. Government Printing Office, 1980.

3

Hearing-Impaired Children from Non-Native-Language Homes

Gilbert L. Delgado

Social, economic, and political factors, augmented by improved transportation, have created population changes and mixes throughout the world. It is reasonable to assume that these population shifts have also occurred in schools and programs for hearing-impaired children in the United States and that increasing numbers of hearing-impaired students come from non-English-speaking homes.

This assumption is borne out by a report that 40 percent of the hearing-impaired students in New York City are Hispanic (Lerman & Fischgrund, 1980). One would expect similar data from other parts of the country, particularly metropolitan areas such as Miami, Chicago, Dallas, and Los Angeles.

In order to obtain basic information on this hypothesis, the Gallaudet Survey of Hearing-Impaired Children from Non-Native-Language Homes was conducted during the 1979–80 academic year. The national survey consisted of a questionnaire sent to 1,203 programs on the mailing list of the Office of Demographic Studies, Gallaudet College. The questionnaire attempted to obtain baseline information, identify special characteristics, note enrollment increases or decreases, and study special accommodations and research needs.

Survey Results

A total of 751 programs (62 percent of those polled) responded to the survey, reporting data on 41,489 hearing-impaired children. (See Table 1 for distribution of programs by size of enrollment.) Of the 41,489

Reprinted with adaptations from *American Annals of the Deaf* (April 1981) by permission of the publisher. Copyright 1981 by Conference of Educational Administrators Serving the Deaf, Inc., and Convention of American Instructors of the Deaf, Inc.

Table 1
Non-Native-Language Survey:
Distribution of Programs by Enrollment Size

Number of Students	Percentage of Programs*
Less than 10	26
10–25	24
26–50	17
51–75	9
76–100	5
101–150	9
151 and above	10
Total	100

*$n = 751$

children enrolled in the programs, 12,237 were reported as having handicaps in addition to hearing impairment. This represents 29 percent of the students in the survey, a figure which agrees with that reported by the Office of Demographic Studies' Annual Survey of Hearing-Impaired Children and Youth (Karchmer, Milone, & Wolk, 1979).

The estimated number of children from non-English-speaking (NES) homes in the Non-Native-Language Survey was 3,011, or 7 percent of the total. Approximately 40 percent of the programs reported at least one child from an NES home. Respondents often were not certain of the language spoken in the home, due to lack of communication with the parents. For example, one school—located in one of the most heavily Hispanic-populated states in the country—reported that it knew of only two students from Spanish-speaking homes. Also in some cases, especially with bilingual parents, two languages apparently were used interchangeably in the home, e.g., English/Spanish. Only one program reported using a language other than English in the classroom.

Of the group of children from NES homes, 1,552 or 51 percent reportedly had handicaps in addition to their hearing loss. This incidence rate is far above the rate for all students surveyed in the 751 programs (see Figure 1, p. 31). Table 2 compares hearing-impaired students in the U.S. reported to the Annual Survey of Hearing-Impaired Children and Youth in 1978–79 with those reported to the Non-Native-Language Survey with regard to specific additional handicaps.

Of interest in Table 2 are the percentages of mentally retarded children, children with emotional or behavioral problems, and those with specific learning disabilities. Note that the reported incidence of

Table 2
Hearing-Impaired Students with Additional Handicaps:
Comparison of Two Surveys

	Percentage of Students	
Additional Handicap	*Non-Native-Language Survey (1979–1980)[a]*	*Annual Survey (1978–1979)[b]*
Mental Retardation	23	7.7
Emotional or Behavioral Disability	23	6.4
Specific Learning Disability	23	5.0[c]
Cerebral Palsy	18	2.7
Legal Blindness or Severe Visual Problem	14	8.1
Orthopedic	14	2.0
Minimal Brain Injury	11	2.4
Heart Disorder	9	2.5
Other	8	1.4
Epilepsy or Convulsive Disorder	2	1.0

Note. Columns add to more than 100 percent due to students with more than one additional handicap.

[a]$n = 41,489$

[b]$n = 53,306$. Unpublished data from the Office of Demographic Studies, Gallaudet College, based on its Annual Survey of Hearing-Impaired Children and Youth, 1978–79.

[c]Estimated; original data included specific learning disability and psychomotor impairment.

Figure 1
Non-Native-Language Survey:
Students with Reported Additional Handicaps

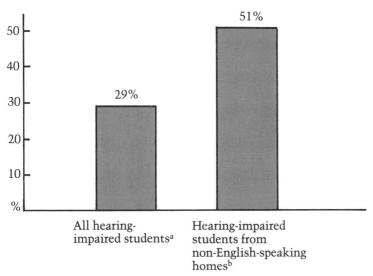

[a]12,237 of 41,489
[b]1,552 of 3,011

these additional handicaps was three to four times higher in the Non-Native-Language Survey than in the annual survey. One suspects that the level of additional handicaps among children from NES homes is inflated by assessment personnel and procedures that are not fully sensitive to non-native language and culture. Insensitivity to these factors can lead to incorrect diagnosis, incorrect educational placement, and faulty teaching strategies used with children from NES homes.

One question on the Non-Native-Language Survey asked if the number of these children in the schools was increasing or decreasing. Fifty-seven percent of the programs reported an increasing number, 35 percent stated the number remained the same, and only 8 percent indicated a decreasing enrollment of children from NES homes.

In regard to academic achievement, each program was asked to compare its students from NES homes with the other students enrolled in the program. A large majority of the programs, 65 percent, indicated that the students from NES homes generally were performing at a lower academic level than their classmates (see Table 3).

Table 3
Non-Native-Language Survey:
Comparative Rating of Academic Acheivement

Academic Achievement of Hearing-Impaired Students from Non-English-Speaking Homes is Rated	Number of Programs*
Better than students from English-speaking homes	51
Equal to students from English-speaking homes	207
Lower than students from English-speaking homes	475

*No response from 18 of the 751 programs.

On the question of language backgrounds of the students, 21 languages other than English were reported. The predominant second language was Spanish, followed by Portuguese, Vietnamese, and several East Indian languages and dialects.

The survey looked at the children's level of adjustment to their various programs. Almost 50 percent of the children for NES homes reportedly had adjusted "well" or "very well." With regard to providing special training and orientation for parents, 32 percent of the programs responded "yes" and 68 percent "no."

Methods and Materials

The survey elicited information on special methods and materials used with these children and their parents. The majority of programs indicated that they provided no bilingual/bicultural or other special programming. Reasons given included the following:

1. The children ultimately will have to integrate into the larger society; hence, emphasis on English language and mainstream culture is more desirable and practical.

2. There are only small numbers of these children; thus special programming is questionable on a cost-effective basis.

3. Respondents have insufficient information on how to begin to serve this population.

Some special approaches and materials were mentioned, however. The following is a list of those methods and materials most often used:

Methods

Special tutoring

Total communication

Cued speech

Bilingual education

—teachers

—resource teachers

—translators for parents

—teacher aides

—volunteers

—parent facilitators

Correspondence, reports, etc., to parents translated into language of the home

Sign books translated into native language and cross-referenced

Second language instructor for children and parents

Use of only native language in first year of school

Utilization of bilingual personnel from regular schools

Children tested in native language

Manual alphabet

Materials

Second languge

Apple Tree Series

Captioned films

Distar Language

Mecham Program

Videotapes

It is significant to note that teaching parents and children sign language and fingerspelling, or total communication via special materials or a bilingual instructor, seemed to provide a medium by which some communication barriers were ameliorated. Respondents felt that sign utilization helped parents to communicate at home with their children and to reinforce, or at least lessen the confusion of, oral communication.

Research

The already large and steadily increasing number of hearing-impaired children from non-native-language homes underlines the need for a great deal of research. Survey respondents highlighted the need for research in four main areas:

Assessment

Measurement of entry language level

Appropriate psychological tests

Hearing tests

Language(s) for instruction

Effectiveness of bilingual instruction and materials

Language

Period of time for use of native language (transition)

Linguistic differences

Cognitive and linguistic development

Impact of sign language

International sign system

Culture

Parent orientation to deafness

Cultural orientation of educational personnel

Impact of culture and religion on student adjustment and educational success

Pluralistic factors

Self-concept

Male/female role

Demography and Law

Population shifts

Laws and regulations affecting mobility

Laws and regulations affecting educational programming (e.g., compulsory native-language mandate)

Many programs have sufficient numbers of children for research purposes; yet only two programs were attempting to find the answers to the growing list of questions. Projecto Oportunidad at the Rhode Island School for the Deaf was and is providing a bilingual/bicultural program for children from Spanish- and Portuguese-speaking homes (Fischgrund, 1980). It employs a Spanish and a Portuguese teacher of the deaf. In addition to bilingual teaching, the project provides training and orientation to parents and serves as a resource center for area programs serving the hearing impaired. A collaborative project is the LISTO (Latino In-Service Training & Orientation) project under supervision of the Lexington School for the Deaf (Lerman & Fischgrund, 1980). LISTO provides training for classroom teachers, Hispanic resource teachers, and social workers/paraprofessionals to work with the large number of Hispanic deaf children in the New York City area. The project also has begun to address needs in the areas of training, support personnel, parent programs, language assessment, analysis, transition, and home maintenance.

The need for appropriately trained professional staff has already been recognized as a high national priority by the Office of Special Education and Rehabilitative Services, U.S. Department of Education; yet, other than the data and information garnered by Projecto Oportunidad and LISTO, there exists no relevant national literature. In addition, a variety of support services are needed for this growing population. These include bicultural orientation for students, staff, and faculty; home visitors as well as orientation and English instruction for parents; bilingual personnel for the intake process; and integration with regular school bilingual programs, to name only a few.

More Effective Programs

The numbers of hearing-impaired children from NES homes clearly are increasing. Substantial numbers of Hispanic children already are enrolled in schools in most regions of the country.* Yet we have virtually no research—and few plans to do research—on the most appropriate way or ways to educate these children.

Other than existing second-language materials, little has been done to address the special problems of this population. Included are issues such as:

1. Should we adhere to preparing all children for the larger society in which they live? Or should our objective be more multicultural?

*Two years after the Non-Native-Language Survey, data from Gallaudet College's Center for Assessment and Demographic Studies (CADS; formerly Office of Demographic Studies) show the continued growth in the number of Hispanic hearing-impaired students. Of the 54,774 hearing-impaired children and youth in CADS' 1981–82 annual survey, 5,185 or 9.5 percent were Hispanic. This is up from 6.8 percent in 1973–74 and 8.5 percent in 1977–78.

This national trend has special impact on particular states and regions. In a separate study of hearing-impaired students in Texas in 1981–82, for example, CADS found that 26 percent (1,154 of 4,363) were Hispanic. In regional day school programs, an average of 28 percent of the students were Hispanic; at the Texas School for the Deaf, 16 percent of the students were Hispanic.

In the Texas survey, nearly 75 percent (859 of 1,154) of the hearing-impaired Hispanic students came from Spanish-speaking homes. This runs counter to the assumption that, as cultural assimilation occurs, the use of non-native language in the home diminishes.

2. Given a "different" culture, religion, and set of values, what are
   reasonable future careers and employment opportunities for these
   children?

   Mandates exist in a growing number of countries to teach children
in their native language. Triggered by the *Lau v. Nichols* case (U.S.
Supreme Court, 1974), California and other states are assessing the
compliance of special education programs with the mandates. In the
Lau case, brought by parents of Chinese children in San Francisco, the
Court observed that Title VI of the Civil Rights Act of 1964 requires
a school to provide "meaningful" education and that such an education is precluded for the student who does not understand the English
language and yet is not provided with special instruction.

   The time has come for educators of deaf children to be aware of the
non-native-language problem as it relates to their special populations
and to work with national, state, and local authorities to conduct
research, develop materials, and implement more effective programs
in this area.

References

Fischgrund, J. E. Projecto Oportunidad. Informal program description,
    Rhode Island School for the Deaf, 1980.

Gentile, A., & McCarthy, B. *Additional handicapping conditions
    among hearing-impaired students, United States: 1971–72* (Series
    D, Number 14). Washington, D.C.: Gallaudet College Office of
    Demographic Studies, 1973.

Karchmer, M. A., Milone, M. N., Jr., & Wolk, S. Educational significance
    of hearing loss at three levels of severity. *American Annals of the Deaf*,
    1979, *124*(2), 97–109.

Karchmer, M. A., Rawlings, B. W., Trybus, R. J., Wolk, S., & Milone, M. N.
    *Educationally significant characteristics of hearing-impaired
    students in Texas, 1977–78* (Series C, Number 4). Washington, D.C.:
    Gallaudet College Office of Demographic Studies, 1979.

Lau v. Nichols, 414 U.S. 563 (1974).

Lerman, A., & Fischgrund, J. *Improving services to Hispanic hearing-
    impaired students and their families.* Paper presented at the 9th
    Annual Meeting of NABE, Anaheim, April 1980.

Luetke-Stahlman, B. A proposed systematic study of language variables in hearing-impaired children from Spanish-speaking homes. Doctoral dissertation proposal, Pennsylvania State University, 1978.

Office of Demographic Studies, Gallaudet College. Unpublished data based on the Annual Survey of Hearing-Impaired Children and Youth, 1978–79.

Ries, P. W., Bateman, D. L., & Schildroth, A. *Ethnic background in relation to other characteristics of hearing-impaired students in the United States* (Series D, Number 15). Washington, D.C.: Gallaudet College Office of Demographic Studies, 1975.

4

Survey of Hispanic Hearing-Impaired Students and Their Families in New York City

Alan Lerman

This survey took place seven years ago and started a series of demonstration and training activities that are still continuing. The general findings for deaf children with first generation mainland parents from Puerto Rico are still valid. While children from second and third generation and/or middle-class-aspiring families have less difficulty being absorbed into the traditional schools, new migrant and immigrant families continue to face problems similar to the survey group. The study set out to document the general needs of this population for the first time, and we have become more aware of the specific needs of Hispanic students and families through subsequent research. However, we still remain in the initial phase of understanding the problems of non-English-speaking and minority status students.

Many educators of the deaf have developed a greater awareness of the needs of special populations. But changes in services for the Hispanic families and children have come more slowly, hampered by the lack of trained personnel and the difficulty of institutional change.

The Survey

In February 1975, after one and a half years of discussion and planning, the CREED VII project was initiated in New York state. Eleven schools for the deaf and blind and the State Education Department agreed to cosponsor the first research and demonstration project of its kind in the United States. The project enlisted the cooperation of three private and two public schools and programs in New York City: Lexington School for the Deaf, JHS-47 School for the Deaf, St. Francis de Sales School for the Deaf, St. Joseph's School for the Deaf, and the Schools for Language and Hearing Impaired Children. We identified a total of 765 children from Hispanic families who were enrolled at the five participating schools. This represented about 50 percent of the total enrollment in the five schools. The survey, completed in 1976, was the first stage of the project that subsequently examined alternative approaches to the education of deaf Hispanic students.

An extremely large number of Spanish-speaking people live in the New York metropolitan area, and increasing numbers of them reside in cities throughout New York state. It is no surprise then that the enrollment of children with Spanish surnames in schools for the deaf has increased dramatically. A disproportionate number of these children are placed in the low-achieving or learning-disabled groups in the schools. In educating this group of children, schools have attempted to deal with problems as they arose. At the time of the survey there had been no systematic attempt to understand the problems and develop resources and programs that could meet these students' needs.

Limited information was available on the academic and affective functioning of Hispanic deaf children. The information indicated that deaf Hispanic children were experiencing academic difficulties (Office of Demographic Studies, 1975; McCahill, 1971; Balick, 1972).

Utilizing the 1973 Stanford Achievement Test, Special Edition for Hearing Impaired Students (SAT-HI), the Office of Demographic Studies found that Spanish-American deaf students had lower achievement levels than white deaf students and, in vocabulary and reading comprehension, lower levels than the other minority groups surveyed (Jensema, 1975). The literature on nonwhite deaf students, hearing Hispanic students on the mainland, and bilingual education research confirmed the need to determine the effectiveness of our education programs for Hispanic students. More specifically, we needed to know to what extent the effectiveness of such programs is influenced by a different language, a different culture, lower socioeconomic status, teaching techniques, and/or staff attitudes.

Goals of the Survey

The purpose of the study was to support the academic and affective functioning of deaf children from Hispanic families living in the New York City metropolitan area. This meant systematically examining the needs of Hispanic children and their families through (a) a survey to determine the linguistic, educational, cultural, demographic, and interpersonal characteristics of—and the social, child care, and educational needs of—the family; and (b) an evaluation of the linguistic, academic, social, and emotional functioning of the child.

We sought to answer the following specific questions:

1. What is the demographic profile of the Hispanic population enrolled in metropolitan New York schools for the deaf?

2. What are the general background characteristics of this population in terms of the home environment, home language, school environment, cultural factors, and factors related to the child's deafness?

3. What are the general characteristics of this population in terms of linguistic and affective functioning in school?

4. Which factors in the Hispanic deaf child's background affect the ability to function in school?

Figure 1
Representation of Deaf Hispanic Child's Language Development

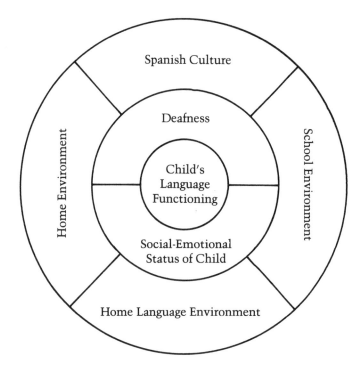

We chose to consider the child's linguistic competence as the central focus in understanding behavior. We then reviewed the major inputs that may affect language functioning. In each of the defined areas we asked, What aspects of this area may specifically influence the child's language behavior? From this approach we devised a series of items that we were able to connect with the central focus (Figure 1). We decided which items were to be obtained through "global ratings," school records, teacher ratings, formal assessments of children, and family interviews.

Language Status of the Child

The child's language functioning was defined in terms of face-to-face communication; competencies in reading and writing were not considered for the purposes of this study. We chose to rate the child's communicative abilities in three areas:

1. Oral English

2. Oral Spanish

3. Oral English combined with some form of manual communication (gestures, formal signs, or fingerspelling)

For each of the three ratings, we further distinguished between the child's receptive and expressive abilities.

Social-Emotional Status of the Child

Four major features were incorporated into our assessment of the child's social-emotional status; they were chosen to reflect the child's degree of success in functioning in an academic setting. The features were

1. Relationships with others

2. Orientation to school tasks

3. Socially disruptive behavior

4. Dependence/independence

We felt that these features would not only influence the child's natural language development but also affect whatever formal language instruction the child would receive in school.

Hispanic Culture

The questions developed by the project were designed to tap the following aspects of the culture/environment: identification with Puerto Rican or other Hispanic national backgrounds, commitment to maintaining the Spanish language in the home, and fatalistic attitudes toward life. These aspects of Hispanic culture had been described as important factors in determining the relative exposures to English and Spanish in nonschool settings (Fishman et al., 1971). Strong identification with Hispanic culture might create difficulties for the child in school activities. For example, the teacher might negatively interpret a child's "culturally appropriate" behavior as "deviant."

Home Environment

The home environment aspect of the model was conceptualized as covering four basic areas:

1. Parents' attitudes toward education and their expectations concerning the child's future

2. The extent to which the family has sought assistance from other institutions

3. The degree of difficulty in maintaining contact between the family and the school.

4. The socioeconomic status of the family

We felt that parental attitudes and expectations would influence the amount of home support for the child's education, thereby indirectly affecting the child's behavior at school. The parents' need for and success with obtaining agency assistance (medical, financial, etc.) may affect the child's functioning. Parents' ability to maintain contact with the educational institution may be related to their attitudes or to aspects of the home situation. The socioeconomic status of the family may influence the child's adjustment to an essentially middle class school environment.

Home Language Environment

Most of the literature indicated the paramount importance of the home language environment to the child's subsequent language competence. Our research focused on items relating to the language sources in the home for the child, the general language environment in the household, the specific nature of the communication with the deaf child, and the attitudes toward English in the family. Identifying information was sought for each of the family members (age, education, place of birth, etc.). Finally, we identified the main communicator and main caregiver in the household, assuming that they would be the two primary language models for the child.

School Environment

Three factors related to school environment were investigated: the child's educational history; programs, policies, or other accommodations instituted by the school specifically to benefit the child; and the teacher's attitude toward, and evaluation and placement of, the Hispanic child in the class.

Deafness

In addition to the direct influences of deafness on a child's language development, we felt that the circumstances surrounding both the discovery of the child's deafness and the reaction to it might influence the child's academic functioning.

Instruments and Sample

In developing the areas of the model, we were concerned with surveying all the major aspects that could affect the child's language functioning. The instruments and materials were developed to provide a broad survey and not an in-depth study of any specific aspect.

The project developed a Language Assessment instrument, a Teacher Rating form, and a Family Interview questionnaire. Observation was limited to the language evaluation conducted by our staff and to limited observations made during the family interviews.

We decided to focus first on children of elementary school age, and we evaluated and interviewed an initial sample of 200 from this group. Prior to the random sampling, four age groupings (6–7, 8–9, 10–11, 12) were formed, and deaf children (hearing loss of 82 dB or greater) were

Table 1
Parental Characteristics

Characteristic	Mother	Father
Parent is present in the home	96%	48%
Parent inaccessible	—	35%
Parent is a hearing person	99%	100%
Median age (in years)	34	39
Born in Puerto Rico	86%	80%
Born in other Hispanic countries	14%	20%
Comes from a rural background	58%	57%
Median time in mainland U.S. (in years)	13	16
Highest education level attained:		
Elementary schooling (0–6 years)	30%	31%
High school (7–12 years)	53%	43%
High school graduate	8%	16%
Some college	3%	4%
Vocational schooling	3%	6%

separated from those enrolled primarily in classes for language-disordered children. The children were also grouped according to sex. The final sample included 188 subjects: 144 deaf and 44 language-disordered children, with equal numbers of children in each age grouping.

The families represented in this group were poor Puerto Rican families from rural backgrounds. Compared with survey information on other Hispanic groups, this group was more severely disabled. In a study by Padilla, Carlos, and Keefe (1976), the majority of the Mexican-American respondents were described as native born, working, married with intact households, and having available kinship groups. By contrast, 48 percent of the Hispanic families of deaf children in our study were on welfare, 83 percent were classified as poverty level, slightly more than half had intact families, and the median educational level of the adults was sixth grade (Tables 1 and 2).

Table 2
Current Status of Families

Characteristic	Percent
Socioeconomic status of household:	
Professional and/or managerial	8
Skilled and/or semi-skilled	30
Unskilled and/or unemployable	62
One or both adults currently employed	37
Family is on welfare	48
Family is classified below poverty level	83
Gets assistance from community agencies	87
Condition of neighborhood:	
Well maintained	17
Changing	26
Deteriorated	57
Grandmother is present in household	5
Child's main caretaker is:	
Father	2
Mother	96
Grandmother	1
Main sibling	1
Number of children in home:	
Only child	7
1–2 siblings	47
3 or more siblings	46
Has other deaf siblings	5

The parents were essentially an immigrant group; 98 percent of them were born in Puerto Rico or other Latin countries. They arrived on the U.S. mainland in their late teens or early twenties. In 35 percent of the families surveyed, the fathers were inaccessible.

In almost all surveyed families the mother was the main caretaker. Most of the families resided in deteriorating neighborhoods. Very few families reported the presence of an available kinship group, and many of the families appeared to be isolated from the social fabric of their community.

Most parents in the survey were brought up in a relatively traditional environment (Table 3). As children, their presence in the midst of adult activities was permitted as long as they did not actively participate. The parents were aware of prejudices, wished to be identified as Puerto Rican, and attended church regularly. The deaf child's home language environment was a mixture of Spanish and English, with Spanish as

Table 3
Selected Responses of Puerto Rican Parents

Parent at present time:	*Percent*
Agrees that Puerto Rican people have it harder here	58
Prefers to be called Puerto Rican (not American)	91
Goes to church regularly	65
Attends Spanish language religious services	66
When parent was a child:	
Was allowed to stay when parents had company	
Always	43
Sometimes	7
Never	50
Was allowed to talk in conversation with company	
Always	37
Sometimes	6
Never	57
Was allowed to contradict parents	
Always	9
Sometimes	10
Never	81

Table 4
Home Language Environment: Media Usage and Interview

Parents and/or Family	Percent
Reads newspapers in:	
Spanish only	29
English only	27
Both Spanish and English	32
Watches TV programs in:	
Spanish	16
English	81
Listens to the radio programs in:	
Spanish	59
English	36
Reads magazines in:	
Spanish only	29
English only	12
Both Spanish and English	30
Spanish used for interview	94
Spanish spoken among family during interview	90
Spanglish/code-switching occurred during interview	25

the dominant spoken language (Table 4). The parents wanted their children to learn Spanish, but they also recognized the importance of English.

In communicating with the deaf child, most parents relied primarily on oral Spanish or a combination of signs and gestures associated with Spanish (Table 5). The main communicator (with the deaf child) was the mother in nearly two out of three homes and one of the deaf child's siblings in most of the other homes. Eighty percent of the mothers and 40 percent of the siblings spoke Spanish only. In contrast, the parents

Table 5
Parent Report of Communication in the Home with Deaf Child

Language Used	Mother to Deaf Child	Father to Deaf Child	Sibling to Deaf Sibling	Deaf Child to Family Members
Mainly oral Spanish	32%	30%	11%	9%
Mainly oral English	10%	13%	15%	9%
Oral English and Spanish	11%	12%	21%	3%
Some manual (with oral language)	42%	44%	50%	75%
Some gestures (with oral language)	5%	1%	3%	4%
Main communicator with deaf child	59%	6%	34%	—
Primarily speaks Spanish	83%	77%	42%	—

reported that 75 percent of the deaf children communicated through manual means; only 9 percent reported deaf children who used oral Spanish.

In the past five to ten years, a number of investigators—working independently and with different premises—have indicated that the quality of the parent-child relationship is ultimately crucial in determining the level of functioning for deaf adults. The deaf Hispanic children we surveyed had a unique problem in this regard. They communicated mostly through signs and gestures to family members who spoke mostly Spanish; this home language conflicted with the English used in their schools. The conflict created greater isolation and more problems in the family relationship than existed in the average deaf child's family.

Language and Affective Functioning

The data on students' Spanish language are not presented. Few students scored above the lowest levels on the test. The extremely limited range of scores meant that this information could not be used in subsequent analyses which examined the relationships between variables. Why did the students appear to have such limited Spanish? Several explanations were offered. One was that the school setting constrained the students from expressing themselves in Spanish, since the school policy was to limit communication to oral English or total communication modes and codes. While the survey could not confirm this, there were instances in which students were informally observed using Spanish with other students or their parents outside the classroom.

Another explanation was that the limited Spanish was due to family communication patterns changing with the child's initial progress in school. Where parents might have communicated in oral Spanish to the deaf child, their awareness of the child's initial acquisition at school of English or sign language (high status languages) led them to return to a simple gestural communication. The "regression" by the parents was a response to their discomfort with the communication codes introduced by the child. The change in communication patterns limited the development of the child's Spanish skills.

The English test scores, while limited, were more varied. The test used was adapted from a test for younger hearing children. It sampled a wide range of expressive and receptive behaviors. A maximum score of 33 represented the level of a well-functioning, normal-hearing 6-year-old student's oral language (Table 6).

The individual student language assessments were conducted by a team of project evaluators at each participating school. Teachers were provided with the same test items and were asked to evaluate the students based on their familiarity with each child's functioning in the classroom. The classroom teachers also evaluated the students using the Social-Emotional Behavior Index developed at the Lexington School (Table 7). Higher scores indicated better adjustment. Finally, teachers rated their students' academic and behavioral functioning (Table 8).

Table 6
Students' English Language Scores by Mode and Rater

| | Students' Rating* by | |
| | Project Evaluators | Classroom Teachers |
Language Mode		
Oral receptive	10.5	3.2
Oral expressive	9.6	1.9
Combined (oral and manual) receptive	17.1	19.5
Combined (oral and manual) expressive	12.4	11.0

*Maximum score of 33.

Table 7
Social-Emotional Behavior Index: Ratings of Deaf Students at Different Ages, Comparing the Hispanic Sample with Previous Pilot Study Sample

Age Group	Mean Scores of Students in Current Study (n = 144)	Mean Scores* of Students in Lexington School Pilot Study (n = 250)
6–7	69	70
8–9	56	64
10–11	48	81
12	40	81

*Includes Lexington children who were in mental health treatment and whose mean scores were 10–20 points below average for pilot group.

Table 8
Teachers' Ratings of Children's General Academic and Behavioral Functioning

Function	Percent of Students
Academic performance is average or above for class	61
Behavioral functioning is average or above for class	76
Child does as well as he or she can	49
Grade level of books child can read in school:	
Reading readiness	24
Primer	36
1st grade	17
2nd grade	21
3rd grade or above	2

While teachers' and evaluators' ratings of students' oral (expressive and receptive) English skills contrasted sharply (Table 6), the general level of language and social-emotional functioning found in the sample confirmed the academic and behavioral difficulties reported in studies of normal-hearing Puerto Rican students. Because the measures reflect the expectations of a middle class, mainstream culture, the results are not surprising.

Some comment should be made on these results. The discrepancies between the teachers' and evaluators' ratings of oral language may be due to the fact that most of the children were in classrooms where total communication was the accepted mode; it was more difficult, therefore, for the teacher to determine the oral language competence separately. This evaluation and the teachers' low estimates of reading competence apparently do not affect the teachers' positive general ratings of the students' academic functioning. Similarly, the lower teacher ratings of children on social-emotional behaviors contrast with their general impressions of relatively adequate behavioral functioning. Because no teacher wishes to stigmatize a child, the teacher will respond to global questions in a more favorable manner. The lesson here is that more specific questions produce clearer information.

Home Environment and Student Functioning

The second phase of the analysis examined the relationships between specific aspects of the model and their influence on the language functioning of the subjects.

This analysis clarified the fact that different schools had different student populations. Within these populations the most highly relevant variables were the presence of the natural father, which changes the socioeconomic level and permits the mother to be more accessible to the child; and the traditional upbringing of the parents, which influences their language usage and their involvement with the child.

If the father is not available, most of the influences on the child's language functioning are related to the mother's ability to cope with her general environment. If the father is available, then other aspects of the household become more important in understanding the child's functioning. The second variable—the degree of tradition in the household—is equally important. Parents from more traditional backgrounds tend to be less involved with the educational needs of the child and more concerned with basic child care.

All family items were examined in relation to the examiner's rating of the child's ability in English and the teacher's rating of the child's social-emotional functioning. We had wished to examine the family background variables in relation to the child's ability in Spanish, but the range of scores was too limited to permit this. Neither measure (language or social-emotional behavior) is sensitive to cultural differences. They rather reflect the middle class, mainstream orientation of the then-existing programs to the students and their families. The schools teach English in their "traditional" ways and expect both children and parents to behave toward the school in the traditional manner. It is not surprising that the more middle class and acculturated the child and family are the better the school does its job of "traditional" teaching. The more acculturated the child, the better he or she appears to meet the middle class standards of behavior.

The following results therefore indicate that children from poorer, less acculturated families show lower English and social-emotional functioning. This points up the mismatch between what the institutions are prepared to teach and what the Hispanic children and families need to obtain full educational services. The fact that poor, recent immigrants do poorly on these measures leads to one of two conclusions for educators: (a) that we must endeavor to make all families middle class and mainstream, *or* (b) that we make deaf education more responsive to the needs of the families we serve.

The major groups of variables and factors that influence language functioning may be outlined as follows:

1. In the intact homes, high English language functioning tends to be associated with
   • mothers from other Hispanic countries (not Puerto Rico)
   • more English spoken in the home
   • more English media used in the home
   • less Spanish spoken in the home
   • mothers who have been in the U.S. longer
   • children with better hearing
   • children with no additional handicaps
   • more contact and positive views toward the school
   • geographic location of the family in New York City
   • children with higher social and emotional scores
   • employment of the father

2. In homes where the father is absent, it appears that the potential positive impact of many of the above factors is reduced. Instead, high English language functioning tends to be more directly related to
   • children with no additional handicaps

- children with higher social and emotional scores
- family economic stability (employed adult in home)

3. The lower English language functioning of deaf children tends to be associated with
   - teachers' ratings of less parental interest in school
   - nonattendance of school activities by parent(s)
   - children starting later in first school
   - less communication with deaf child
   - more agency contact
   - more welfare
   - lower socioeconomic status
   - shorter time in New York

Because many of the parents come from rural backgrounds in Puerto Rico, they face a triple problem of acculturation to our current school system. Language, culture, and class differences need to be dealt with by the parents. Many of them feel isolated in the new environment; they find no community support to help them negotiate these differences. Their transition is abrupt and hard. The parents are ill-prepared to deal with the demands that are placed on them and their children. Lack of community support and being poor force parents to expend most of their energy in survival. The factors that appear to be associated with higher English functioning (within our present system) are not available to many parents.

Implications of the Study

Differences in language, cultural background, and socioeconomic level help create barriers to participation in the educational system for the Hispanic deaf student. The system must do its part in adapting to these differences. Changes in instructional activities and in home-school relationships may be required. Reviews of culturally and linguistically sensitive areas such as intake procedures, language assessment, and instruction and curriculum content must be conducted to determine their relevance for Hispanic students.

The assumptions for current family-school activities and relations need further examination. For example, do teachers assume that each family will be able to assist the child at home in learning specific academic skills? What demands can realistically be placed on a single parent struggling to survive in a ghetto environment? To what degree can the school assist a single parent trying to raise a deaf child? This examination may lead to changes in specific services, methods of service delivery, and the nature of parent-school relationships.

In order to consider the needs and make the appropriate changes, the school staff must be prepared for the acquisition of special personnel and the inservice training of current administrators, supervisors, support staff, and classroom teachers. New information and skills may be required and attitudes may have to be changed so that we are better able to understand and deal with the difficulties that these students face.

References

Anastasi, A., & Cardaso, F. (Eds.). *Puerto Rican children in mainland schools.* Metuchen, N.J.: Scarecrow Press, 1968.

Anastasi, A., & DeJesus, C. Language development and non-verbal IQ of Puerto Rican preschool children in New York City. *Journal of Abnormal Psychology,* 1953, *48,* 357–366.

Anderson, G.B., & Bowe, F.G. Racism within the deaf community. *American Annals of the Deaf,* 1972, *117, 617–619.*

Angel, F. Social class or culture? A fundamental issue in the education of culturally different students. In B. Spolsky (Ed.), *The language education of minority children.* Rowley, Mass.: Newbury House, 1972.

Balick, S. (Ed.). *Proceedings of a seminar on speech and hearing sciences for the Hispanic consumer.* New York: Columbia University School of Public Health, 1972.

Bowe, F. Deafness and mental retardation. In J.D. Schein (Ed.), *Education and rehabilitation of deaf persons with other disabilities.* New York: New York University Press, 1974.

Bowe, F.G. Educational, psychological, and occupational aspects of the non-white deaf population. *American Annals of the Deaf,* 1971, *116,* 357–361.

Bucchioni, E. *Home atmosphere and success in school: A sociological analysis of Puerto Rican children.* Unpublished doctoral dissertation, New School for Social Research, New York, 1965.

Cordaso, F. The Puerto Rican child in the American school. *Journal of Negro Education*, 1967, *36*, 181–186.

Cortes, C. A bicultural process for developing Mexican American heritage curriculum (Multilingual Assessment Project: Riverside Component). In A. Castaneda, M. Ramirez, & L. Harold (Eds.), *Systems and Evaluations in Education, 1971–72 Annual Report*. Riverside, Calif., 1972.

Draper, J.F., & Green, D.R. (Eds.). *Exploratory studies of bias in achievement tests*. Monterey, Calif.: McGraw-Hill, 1972.

Dravininkas, S. Educational problems and programs for the Spanish bilingual child. *DCCD Bulletin*, 1975, *12*, 47–54.

Fishman, J., Cooper, R., & Ma, R. *Bilingualism in the barrio*. Bloomington: Indiana University Press, 1971.

Gray, L. Puerto Ricans are the poorest of the poor. *Latin New York*, 1976, *41*, 24–25.

Houston, S.H. A reexamination of some assumptions about the language of the disadvantaged child. *Child Development*, 1970, *41*, 947–961.

Jensema, C. *The relationship between academic achievement and the demographic characteristics of hearing impaired youth*. Washington, D.C.: Gallaudet College Office of Demographic Studies, 1975.

Lentgerg, M.J. *The ethnic student: Academic and social problems*. Paper presented at the annual convention of the American Psychological Association, Honolulu, September 1972.

McCahill, P. A case of disinterest: The deaf in Puerto Rico. *American Annals of the Deaf*, 1971, *116*, 413–414.

Office for Civil Rights. *Task force findings specifying remedies available for eliminating past educational practices ruled unlawful under Lau vs. Nichols*. Washington, D.C.: Department of Health, Education, and Welfare, 1975.

Office of Demographic Studies, Gallaudet College. *Ethnic background in relation to other characteristics of hearing impaired students in the United States* (Series D, No. 15). Washington, D.C.: Author, 1975.

Padilla, A.M., & Ruiz, R.A. *Latino mental health: A review of literature*. Washington, D.C.: U.S. Government Printing Office, 1973.

Padilla, A.M., Carlos, M.L., & Keefe, S.E. Mental health service utilization by Mexican Americans. In M.R. Miranda (Ed.), *Psychotherapy with the Spanish-speaking: Issues in research and service delivery* (Monograph No. 3). Los Angeles: UCLA Spanish Speaking Mental Health Research Center, 1976.

Williams, M.W. *Race, poverty, and educational achievement in an urban environment.* Paper presented at the annual convention of the American Psychological Association, Honolulu, September 1972.

The Language Dynamics

5

The Hearing-Impaired Hispanic Child: Sociolinguistic Considerations

Craig Carlisle Dean

The Hispanic population in the United States constitutes the largest and fastest growing minority group with a population approximating 14 million (U.S. Department of Commerce, 1981). Throughout history the Hispanic people have resisted attempts made by the politico-educational system of the United States to assimilate their culture and language (Horner, 1973). Although for many years Spanish was a forbidden language in the schools, large proportions of the Spanish-surnamed population in the United States continue to use their native language and follow the traditions of their culture. This resistance to cultural assimilation has increased in recent years, and a growing awareness of linguistic and cultural identity has spurred a demand for equal opportunities in the areas of education and employment. However, despite several legislative gains and consistent attempts at procuring an equal stance in the American social and economic establishment, the Hispanic population is still a victim of under-education and under-employment (Splintered America, 1980).

Within this Hispanic minority group exists yet another minority population: hearing-impaired children from Spanish-speaking homes. Jensema (1975) reported that 2,650 Hispanic children attended mainland U.S. programs for the hearing impaired. In Texas 25 percent of the children in programs for the hearing impaired were Hispanic, and Spanish was the language most frequently used in 19 percent of the homes of these children (Trybus et al., 1978).

In the years since these studies were completed, there is evidence that growing numbers of children from non-English-speaking (NES) homes are enrolling in programs for the hearing impaired. Fifty-seven percent of the programs in which minority students are enrolled

Adapted from an unpublished paper written by Ms. Dean, a teacher of the hearing impaired, when she was at Texas Women's University.

reported increasing enrollment of children from NES homes; yet only one program indicated that its students were receiving some instruction in their native language (Delgado, 1981).

Three points must be emphasized: The Spanish-speaking population of the U.S. is growing at an increasing rate; a significant number of hearing-impaired children in the U.S. come from homes where Spanish is the primary language; and awareness of the special needs of these children is seriously lacking.

Several studies (Jensema, 1975; Cortez, 1975; Delgado, 1981) have noted that Hispanic deaf children receive significantly lower scores in tests of language development, computation, and social-emotional status than their non-Hispanic peers. However, little research has been conducted to discover the most appropriate method to use in educating these children (Delgado, 1981). It might be helpful to touch upon the characteristics of the various sociocultural and linguistic dynamics existing in the environments of hearing-impaired children from NES homes.

The first purpose of this paper is to review the literature in the areas of bilingual education, language acquisition, and hearing impairment relevant to determining the validity of implementing a bilingual/bicultural component into the hearing-impaired Hispanic child's educational program. The second purpose is to discuss the many factors to be considered in designing such a program.

Bilingual Education in the U.S.

Mercer (1972) found that a disproportionately large number—in fact a majority—of school-age Hispanic children had been classified as academically retarded and culturally deprived. Professionals believed that this developmental delay was attributable to the Hispanic child's linguistic and cultural diversity. Parents, educators, and legislators attacked the problem of dual language exposure. One result was the Bilingual Education Act, which theoretically ensured that children from NES homes would be educated, at least to some degree, in the language of the home.

The linguistic theory espoused by proponents of bilingual education proposes that children whose dominant language is not English will learn English with more facility if first their native language is developed as the basic means of communication. If Hispanic children are given the opportunity to develop their oral and written Spanish skills, this language base ultimately will make the acquisition of

English a smoother process (Saville-Troike, 1977; Thonis, 1977). The sociolinguistic theory emphasizes the role that language plays in the development of the child's self-concept and attitude toward language and culture. A bilingual program, it was believed, must also be a bicultural program, helping children to appreciate their natural heritage (Saville-Troike, 1977). The cognitive theory behind bilingual education states that a child's first language is accompanied by the expansion of conceptual powers. A child who has internalized one language can then more readily grasp new concepts. When a second language is introduced, new linguistic rules are used to express concepts that the child has already assimilated through the first language (Saville-Troike, 1977).

Research conducted in the areas of self-concept, cognitive development, and language learning as they relate to bilingual/bicultural education appears to be conclusive in the first two instances and inconclusive in the latter. Studies evaluating the relationship between instruction in one's native language and development of a positive self-concept indicate that those Hispanics who participated in a bilingual/bicultural program felt better about themselves and had a more positive attitude toward their school experiences than did the control subjects (Cohen, 1973; Segalowitz, 1978). And studies designed to show the relationship between the development of cognition and bilingual/bicultural education indicate a positive influence on the development of concept formation by early instruction in one's native language (Modiano, 1966; Wilson, 1973). But the empirical evidence is contradictory in terms of a linguistic justification for bilingual education (Paulston, 1974). Several bilingual programs were reportedly effective; student progress in second language learning was better than the progress obtained through a more traditional curriculum (Inclán, 1977; Modiano, 1966). However, one well-known study (Lambert & Tucker, 1977) does not support the merits of native language instruction. The children participating in this program were instructed exclusively in the second language except for two daily half-hour periods of language arts in their native language. Their skills in both languages were no lower than the control group's skills.

Paulston (1974) attempts to explain the conflicting nature of the empirical evidence as a reflection more on the paucity of such studies than on the linguistic merits of the program. In reviewing the research data, she claims that language was not the only causal variable in successful school achievement. The social situation of the community in which the bilingual program existed and the positive attitude of the parents and teachers toward the program could effect improved school achievement more than the specific nature of the language instruction. Thus, in order to explain the success or failure of a bilingual program, one must look beyond linguistic factors to the socioeconomic and cultural background of the non-English-speaking child and the function of the native and second languages in the community. It seems safe to say that those children who come from middle class homes where the native language is valued and the second language is encouraged—and who are participating in a program with well-trained teachers and good materials—will do well in acquiring the second language regardless of the method used, whether it be immediate and complete immersion in the second language or bilingual instruction.

The Hearing-Impaired Hispanic Child

The findings above also apply to the education of the hearing-impaired child from a non-English-speaking home. Several parallels between the hearing Hispanic and the hearing-impaired Hispanic will be discussed in the remainder of this paper.

Is the hearing-impaired Hispanic child affected by the linguistic and cultural duality of his/her world? To what extent, if any, does this duality interfere with the child's social, academic, and linguistic development? As noted earlier, school-age Hispanic children as a whole have produced lower achievement test scores than the Anglo school-age population. The same trend may be observed with hearing-impaired Hispanics and hearing-impaired Anglos. In 1975, the first major, funded project to address the needs of Hispanic deaf children in the United States was established. The project, entitled CREED VII, explored the needs of New York City Hispanic school children who were hearing impaired and language delayed (see chapter 4). The survey indicated that the Hispanic deaf children typically received lower scores than non-Hispanic deaf peers in the areas of language, academic achievement, and social-emotional status (Cortez, 1975).

Jensema (1975) reported that scores on the Stanford Achievement Test for the Hearing Impaired (SAT-HI) were higher for Anglos than for minority students. Performance scores for both groups are provided in Table 1.

Delgado conducted a survey of hearing-impaired children from non-native-language homes (see chapter 3). Sixty-five percent of the programs with children from NES homes indicated that these students were performing at a lower academic level than their classmates. Fifty-one

Table 1
SAT-HI Performance Scores
of Anglo and Hispanic Hearing-Impaired Students

	Mean Score	
Test	*Anglo*	*Hispanic*
Vocabulary	.13	− .35
Reading	.20	− .46
Math	.20	− .39

Note. From *The Relationship Between Academic Achievement and the Demographic Characteristics of Hearing-Impaired Children and Youth,* by C. Jensema, p. 10. Copyright 1975 by Gallaudet College. Reprinted by permission.

percent or 1,552 of the children from NES homes reportedly had handicaps in addition to hearing-impairment. The nature of these statistics makes one question the appropriateness of the assessment tools used as well as the educational placement and teaching strategies.

Socioeconomic Considerations

Why are hearing-impaired Hispanic children receiving low scores and what can be done about it? Several areas of the socioeconomic environment of these children must be explored in order to clarify the factors contributing to their poor academic achievement.

As mentioned, initial language instruction in a student's native language is not necessarily equivalent to a successful bilingual program. Personal and social factors appear to exert a profound influence on the success or failure of bilingual instruction; the social class of the students plays a very dominant role (Paulston, 1974). Likewise, the CREED VII study demonstrated that hearing-impaired Hispanic children from impoverished, monolingual families did not do as well as such children from middle class, assimilated families (Cortez, 1975).

One educator, concerned with training teachers of the minority-group hearing impaired, prepared a handbook on the preparation of personnel involved with educating Hispanic hearing-impaired children (Grant, 1972). She identified several cultural, economic, and geographic conditions of lower-class Hispanic families that appeared to influence the kind of education their children were receiving. Many of the families could not easily afford appropriate medical attention; thus the identification of a hearing loss may have been delayed for a number of years. Clinics had few Spanish-speaking doctors or nurses, so parents were not truly cognizant of their child's hearing problem and its far-reaching consequences. This delayed identification of a hearing loss can be responsible for much of the language delay of hearing-impaired children. Critical periods exist for the acquisition of language; the specific ability for developing language skills peaks around the third or fourth year of life (Moores, 1978). If the child is receiving no amplification, many linguistic cues are not being received.

Dual Language and Speech Exposure

The relationship between various degrees of hearing loss and their imposition upon a child's ability to acquire two separate linguistic codes is a largely unexplored area. Under what conditions can bilingual education benefit a child whose hearing loss imposes great difficulty in the development of just *one* language? By the same token, how might dual language exposure benefit a child with only a slight hearing loss? Much more research is necessary before such questions can be answered. A brief discussion of the processes involved in language acquisition, however, might be helpful in appreciating the scope of the dilemma.

Simply expressed, the child who is acquiring a language is receiving signals from the external world, abstracting common features in the signals, and organizing a system on the basis of these features. Language is produced according to this system. These principles apply as well to the hearing-impaired child who decodes linguistic messages received through the visual, acoustic, and tactile sensory modes.

A Hispanic hearing-impaired child may be receiving Spanish phonologic, syntactic, and semantic cues at home (along with some form of family gesture system) and English phonologic, syntactic, and semantic cues in the school (perhaps coupled with a structured sign system). How effective is the brain in organizing this constant flow of contradictory linguistic codes that are being received by impaired auditory senses? Two systems of rules governing the grammatical structure of utterances and the syntax of sentences must be generated by the brain. For Hispanic hearing-impaired children this creates obvious problems, as indicated by their low achievement scores in the development of communication skills (Cortez, 1975; Delgado, 1981).

Considerations in Developing a Language Program

It is not difficult—although it can be mind-boggling— to imagine the many combinations of receptive, expressive, written, oral, and visual languages to which hearing-impaired Hispanic children are or can be exposed between the home and the school. Developing a language program which uses any number of these combinations to facilitate the child's language learning is a challenging affair. The home and community linguistic environment in which the child lives, the parents' goal for the child and their attitude toward Spanish and English, the range of expressive and receptive language skills the child demonstrates in Spanish and English, and the degree and nature of the child's hearing loss all might be considered while constructing an appropriate communication program.

The type of linguistic environment that exists in the home may vary greatly and will affect the hearing-impaired Hispanic child's dual language skills. Bolen (1980) identified the following possible linguistic situations:

1. Spanish-primary
   English-secondary (little general knowledge)

2. Spanish-primary
   English-secondary (confident in English, but preference for Spanish)

3. Mixed dominance (no preference; switches from one language to another)

4. English-primary
   Spanish-secondary (confident in Spanish, but preference for English)

5. English-primary
   Spanish-secondary (little general knowledge)

Fostering parent-child communication should be a major goal in developing a language program for the child (Liben, 1978; Schlesinger, 1978; Van Uden, 1979). Hearing-impaired children from English-speaking homes typically experience a social deprivation that can be traced to differences in communication between the parents and the child (Liben, 1978). In one study it was found that manual communication used by anyone other than the deaf child occurred in only 12 percent of the hearing families with a deaf child, and, when mothers of deaf children were asked about child-rearing problems, more than half mentioned problems in communication (Schlesinger & Meadow,

1972). In the Spanish-speaking or bilingual home, even further rifts in communication may be provoked if the child's home language is not fostered in the school.

The attitude of the parents toward the first and second language is important in deciding upon a language program (Bolen, 1980). Parental attitudes have played a large role in determining the relative success of bilingual programs developed for hearing children. In identifying the language(s) they want their child to learn, parents must ask themselves what they are prepared to do to provide the optimum language environment in the home. Their own skills in both languages must also be considered.

Could the use of sign language at home and at school serve to alleviate the difficulties resulting from exposure to two distinct oral languages? Delgado found that communication barriers lessened when parents as well as children were taught sign language, fingerspelling, or total communication (see chapter 3). Another factor which would seem to enhance the role of Hispanic parents in the language development of their hearing-impaired child is that certain syntactic structures in American Sign Language and Spanish are similar (Luetke, 1976). For example, the two languages have the same noun-adjective construction (shoes new) and inverted question form (want you drive?).

Upon entering school, what is the extent of the child's English and Spanish language skills and how can this information be used to help determine the feasibility of a bilingual program placement? If the child is a recent immigrant who is mildly hearing impaired, for example, he or she may have already mastered a great deal of the Spanish language. Perhaps he or she is ready for a bilingual approach that emphasizes a slow transition to English, accompanied by a Spanish maintenance component. Speculating on a different situation, a child who demonstrates poor Spanish language skills may not benefit from an immediate English immersion program. The basic tenet of bilingual education is that second-language learning will occur with greater facility once the first language has been acquired.

It is an understatement to say that hearing-impaired children do not acquire their first language by the time they begin schooling. In those studies in which total immersion in the second language proved successful (Lambert & Tucker, 1977), the hearing subjects had already acquired their native language. When a hearing-impaired child comes from a Spanish-speaking home with little language, the wise course of action might be to nurture what little linguistic knowledge the child does possess in the native language before exposing him or her to another language that may not be used in the home.

Other areas in the child's educational program play an integral role in the development of language. The type and degree of the language used to foster the child's reading and speech skills, for example, will influence language skills. Thus the language(s) used to develop these other skill areas should be chosen carefully.

It appears that the most important point that can be gleaned from the few studies of bilingual programs and those conducted on hearing-impaired children from Spanish-speaking homes is that there is no one appropriate language program designed to fulfill the needs of all these children. Language does not exist by itself; it functions as a link between the child's expressive and receptive self and environment. Therefore, one must look at the nature of this function for the particular child; one must note how the child uses language to interact with the world.

Between the Extremes

The following hypothesis is proposed: The hearing-impaired child who is exposed only to Spanish at home should receive intensive Spanish language exposure, at least for the first year of school. Due to the limitations imposed by the hearing loss, all linguistic cues should be in the same language. Parent-child communication is of the utmost importance in the early years of the child's life, so the language of the parents should be reinforced in the school. An alternative hypothesis follows: The hearing-impaired Hispanic child should be exposed only to English from the onset of schooling. A hearing-impaired child from an English-speaking home has enough difficulty trying to master English; if the Hispanic hearing-impaired child is to learn the language of this country, he or she should be exposed to it exclusively from the beginning.

Somewhere between these two extremes is a place for each hearing-impaired child—a place that recognizes each child's unique combination of individual and family/community characteristics.

References

Bolen, D. *The hearing-impaired child from the bilingual home.* Paper presented at meeting of the A.G. Bell Association, Houston, June 1980.

Cortez, E. Meeting the needs of Hispanic deaf children. *The Lexington Reports* (Lexington School for the Deaf), 1975.

Delgado, G. Hearing-impaired children from non-native language homes. *American Annals of the Deaf*, 1981, *126*, 118–121. An adaptation of the article may be found on pages 28–36.

Fishman, J. Bilingualism, intelligence, and language. *Modern Language Journal*, 1965, *49*, 227–237.

Grant, J. *Proceedings of a workshop on the preparation of personnel in the education of bilingual hearing-impaired children, ages 0–4.* San Antonio: Trinity University, 1972.

Horner, J. Bilingualism and the Spanish-speaking child. In F. Williams (Ed.), *Language and poverty: Perspectives of a theme.* New York, Academic Press, 1970.

Inclán, R. Bilingual schooling in Dade County. In W. Mackey & T. Andersson (Eds.), *Bilingualism in early childhood.* Rowley, Mass.: Newbury House, 1977.

Jensema, C. *The relationship between academic achievement and the demographic characteristics of hearing-impaired children and youth* (Series R, No. 2). Washington, D.C.: Gallaudet College Office of Demographic Studies, 1975.

Lambert, W., & Tucker, R. A home/school language switch program. In W. Mackey & T. Andersson (Eds.), *Bilingualism in early childhood.* Rowley, Mass.: Newbury House, 1977.

Liben, L. The development of deaf children: An overview of issues. In L. Liben (Ed.), *Deaf children: Developmental perspectives.* New York: Academic Press, 1978.

Ling, D. *Speech and the hearing-impaired child: Theory and practice.* Washington, D.C.: Alexander Graham Bell Association for the Deaf, 1976.

Luetke, B. Questionnaire results from Mexican-American parents of hearing-impaired children in the United States. *American Annals of the Deaf*, 1976, *121*, 565–568.

Luetke-Stahlman, B. *Similarities in hearing and hearing-impaired linguistic minorities.* Omaha: University of Nebraska at Omaha, 1982.

Mercer, J. *Implication of current assessment procedures for Mexican-American children.* Los Angeles: National Dissemination and Assessment Center, 1978.

Modiano, N. *A comparative study of two approaches to the teaching of reading in the national language.* Unpublished paper, New York University, 1966.

Moores, D. *Educating the deaf: Psychology, principles, and practices.* Boston: Houghton Mifflin, 1978.

Paulston, C. *Implications of language learning theory for language planning: Concerns in bilingual education.* Arlington, Va.: Center for Applied Linguistics, 1974.

Saville-Troike, M. *Linguistic bases for bilingual education.* Los Angeles: National Dissemination and Assessment Center, 1977.

Segalowitz, N. Psychological perspectives on bilingual education. In B. Spolsky & R. Cooper (Eds.), *Frontiers of bilingual education.* Rowley, Mass.: Newbury House, 1978.

Schlesinger, H. The acquisition of bimodal language. In I. M. Schlesinger and L. Namir (Eds.), *Sign language of the deaf: Psychological, linguistic, and sociological perspectives.* New York: Academic Press, 1978.

Schlesinger, H., & Meadow, K. *Sound and sign.* Berkeley: University of California Press, 1972.

Splintered America: Peril or promise. *U.S. News and World Report,* July 10, 1980, pp. 33–37.

Thonis, E. *The dual language process in young children.* Los Angeles: National Dissemination and Assessment Center, 1977.

Trybus, R., Rawlings, B., & Johnson, R. *State survey of hearing-impaired children and youth: A new approach to statewide planning, monitoring, and evaluation of special education programming* (Series C, No. 2). Washington, D.C.: Gallaudet College Office of Demographic Studies, 1978.

U.S. Department of Commerce. *Statistical abstract of the United States.* Washington, D.C.: Bureau of the Census, 1981.

Van Uden, A. Hometraining service for deaf children in the Netherlands. In A. Simmons-Martin & D. Calvert (Eds.), *Parent-infant intervention: Communication disorders.* New York: Grune & Stratton, 1979.

Wilson. Assumptions for bilingual instruction in the primary grades of Navajo schools. In P. Turner (Ed.), *Bilingualism in the Southwest.* Tucson: University of Arizona Press, 1973.

6

Bilingual Problems of the Hispanic Deaf

Harriet Green Kopp

To consider bilingualism and deafness first requires that a distinction be made between the common use of the term *bilingual* as applied to individuals from particular ethnic/cultural groups and *bilingual* in its derivative meaning. If *bilingual* denotes an individual equally fluent in two languages then, by definition, there is no difficulty linguistically or cognitively in relation to input or output in either language. Those adults who, as children, were educated in Euopean countries or grew up near European borders are often multilingual. They can think in more than one language and switch without effort from one language to another. To think in a language is different from having to translate from one language to another. That is, the ability to switch instantly into the storage/associative areas for the language perceived—and to generate the psycholinguistic processing required to provide appropriate output in that language—is usually possible only to those who are native speakers or who have acquired the second language at an early age.

Later second-language learners fluent in reading and speaking often appear to translate second language input into the primary language, process the content, generate the response, and then translate the response back into the second language. Despite the incredible speed at which the cortex can process language, processing differences have been noted between the true bilingual and the second-language learner. People who became fluent in a second language in later childhood or early teens appear to use processing strategies related to the right hemisphere, with some limitation in the integration of the segmental, suprasegmental, and semantic features of the language (Ben Zeev, 1972;

This chapter and chapter 14 are expansions of a paper prepared for the International Congress on Education of the Deaf, Hamburg, West Germany, August 4–8, 1980 (Kopp, 1982, pp. 186–188).

Lambert, 1969; Ojemann & Whitaker, 1978; Sussman, Franklin & Simon, 1982). People who are bilingual from early childhood seem to process language semantically, with a predominant left hemisphere approach (Vaid & Lambert, 1979).

It is significant that so little is known about the neuroanatomical bases for bilingual versus monolingual language processing (Obler, Zatorre, Galloway, & Vaid, 1982). There is some indication that, in true bilinguals, there may be sites within a hemisphere common to both languages as well as separate sites for each language (Albert & Obler, 1978; Ojemann & Whitaker, 1978). Learning two languages simultaneously constitutes a heavy cognitive load in perception and differentiation of input stimuli, association of meaning, organization of storage strategies by acquisition of linguistic and phonologic rules, retrieval from the appropriate storage bank, and generation of output. The level of research does not permit us to do more than speculate about the relative complexity of learning two vastly different languages, such as Chinese and English, compared with two languages having more common ancestry and components. Nor do we know the extent to which the two cortical hemispheres collaborate during the learning period. Observation provides evidence that, after two or three languages have been acquired at an early age, the acquisition of additional languages appears to be facilitated. It is probable that strategies are developed for processing, storage, and retrieval that can be applied across even relatively dissimilar languages.

The term *bilingual* is applied appropriately to hearing, fluent, non-native speakers of a second language. However, it is frequently also used for those who may be fluent in their native language but have only limited fluency in the second language. In the Southwest that primary (native, first) language is often Spanish, in various dialects depending upon the geographic/cultural region. In parts of California it may be Chinese, Japanese, Vietnamese, Thai, or Tagalog. In parts of Florida or New York, it may be Cuban or Puerto Rican Spanish. Too often, individuals classified as ethnic/cultural bilinguals are really monolingual; the second language neither provides fluent communication nor is it usable without internal translation to and from the native tongue.

One additional observation should be made. Most languages were, by origin, based on aural/oral transmission. Later graphic representation attempted to portray acoustic information by abstract symbols. Over time, those symbols have not been subject to the same degree and kind of modification as have their spoken analogs. Thus, the language which we read and write often has not kept pace with the phonetic and phonologic changes of the spoken language. This is especially true of much of our English orthography, which reflects original, historical spellings and pronunciations rather than current oral language. The complex spelling rules and their exceptions do not make English an easy primary or secondary language to read, write, or speak without intensive acoustic input.

Cognitive Load

Although it has not been customary to consider deaf individuals as bilingual, the cognitive task imposed by either concomitant or serial acquisition of sign language and the language of the majority hearing culture is more complex than that faced by the hearing bilingual. In addition, there are particular cognitive problems resulting from differences in the receptive and expressive modes of sign versus spoken language. These differences are significantly greater than the linguistic and phonologic variations observed between such widely disparate languages as Chinese and English. The deaf individual from a Spanish-speaking home who is required to learn English may more appropriately be categorized as trilingual (sign, Spanish, English) than bilingual. If the deaf individual is to be truly bi- or trilingual, the mode (oral/aural/sign/fingerspelling) by which information is transmitted and perceived requires the rapid cognitive processing of diverse code systems. The hearing individual is not subjected to modal problems of comparable difficulty.

Oral/Aural Codes

Some hearing-impaired individuals acquire English as a first language through oral/aural input supported by speechreading. Although speechreading is a visual representation of acoustic output, the two codes lack a one-to-one correspondence. The acoustic input code requires rapid processing of serially perceived stimuli: segmental features (phonemes, blends, syllables, transitional junctures between adjoining sounds, phonemic variations within a speaker and among speakers); and supra segmental features (inflection changes, intonation patterns, melodic patterns, phrasing, loudness, rate) which add emotional and second-order, nonliteral meaning to the articulated phonemic input. When this input is distroted by being filtered through a hearing loss or hearing aid, it is only the redundancy of speech (with consequent opportunities for auditory closure) that permits intelligibility. The accompanying visual input from speechreading is coded differently and perceived serially as sequential movements of articulators and facial muscles. The listener must integrate acoustic and visual information codes that are perceived simultaneously by different organic receptors and processed through different cognitive systems. Oral/motor output, when developed, will be related to the acoustic/visual input, although it will also be monitored in part by kinesthetic feedback.

Visual Codes

Many hearing-impaired individuals acquire their primary language through a system of signs that may constitute a unique language such as American Sign Language (Bellugi, 1980; Bellugi & Studdert-Kennedy, in press) or may be modified to be grammatically analogous to the native spoken language. These signed language components are produced by standardized movements and shapes of the hands accompanied by facial and body cues that add significantly to meaning. Variations within signs are comparable in qualitative differentiation to the variations characteristic of spoken language. However, there is no direct, integral relationship between the acoustic components of oral language and the language of signs. Therefore, speech accompanied by a simultaneously signed message requires the speaker/signer to produce a message in two different symbol systems which may be received by the listener as three separate and distinct language codes: sign, speechreading, acoustic. The three codes are perceived by two receptive organs. The eye perceives sign and speechreading, two vastly different codes. The aided ear perceives the acoustic signal. The complexity of the cognitive processing load is evident for the oral speaker who signs simultaneously and for the hearing-impaired listener/viewer who receives the message.

In transmission of language through fingerspelling, words are literally spelled by an arbitrary coded alphabet. The sequential movement provides a one-to-one correspondence with the graphic alphabet but not with oral output codes. Reception requires visual processing of rapid sequential movements often accompanied by speech and facial or body cues. A combination of sign and fingerspelling is not uncommon because fingerspelling can be used to clarify ambiguous and/or significant ideas. In such cases, two variant visual codes may be alternated. If ASL and fingerspelling are used alternatively for passages in running speech, the different linguistic bases and code systems require a rapid processing shift by both sender and receiver.

Transmission Modes

The mode by which language is transmitted must be considered in addition to the language transmitted. If the language is ASL and both sender and receiver communicate in sign, communication is monolingual and transmission via a visual mode incorporates a single symbol system. However, if a message is transmitted in part through ASL and in part through standard spoken English, the receiver must interpret ASL sign alternated with or accompanied by standard English acoustic/visual input. The redundancy afforded by the additional cues may be either supportive or distracting depending upon the skill levels of sender and receiver. The requisite cognitive processing task is clearly bilingual as well as multimodal.

The use of vision to perceive a language code designed for oral/aural transmission is, at best, difficult. Assessment of the cognitive load on the immature processing system of a young child during the period of initial language acquisition requires careful analysis of the cognitive tasks implicit in the transmission modes and language systems to which the child is exposed. At issue is whether the initial transmission mode or modes and the primary language learned exert a significant effect upon the ability to acquire the target language and to use additional transmission modes. It would appear that, if the initial language is significantly different from the target language, the deaf individual may be effectively bilingual, monolingual, or nonfluent. This depends on familial, educational, physical, and psychosocial variables. The nature of the bilingual cognitive load varies if the original and target languages are ASL and English rather than Spanish and English but, in either case, there are clearly two languages.

For the deaf, a significant bilingual transmission problem resides in the fact that manual communication input/output code systems are quite different from the oral/aural codes. These separate visual/aural/motor systems may be developed at varying levels of fluency and may serve either to reinforce communication or to set up distortion or interference circuits. For example, fluent manual transmission does not provide direct reinforcement of such oral language skills as articulation and phonation.

Simultaneous communication (sometimes called total communication) requires the sender to process two separate motor output codes simultaneously: speech and manual sign or fingerspelling. The deaf receiver must process acoustic and visual input perceived simultaneously in three different codes: acoustic, manual, and speechreading. To date, fluency in simultaneous communication has not been assessed with respect to the cognitive load imposed by simultaneous transmission of its components or the effect of simultaneous reception of competing input codes on psycholinguistic processing at various age and language fluency levels.

When primary language exposure is in Spanish or any other non-English language and the target language is English, problems in linguistic and phonologic acquisition in both the first and second languages may be exacerbated by the particular combination of transmission modes selected. For instance, oral speech output is facilitated by early amplification and the maximal use of residual hearing. If the auditory stimulus at home is in Spanish and at school is in English, opportunities for input/output confusion are even more probable among the hearing impaired than the hearing.

Primary Language and the Home

If the deaf child comes from a family in which English is a second language, the child's linguistic competency may vary in relation to the parents' fluency in their language of choice as well as their skill in using the selected transmission mode or modes. It is essential that the family be encouraged to provide early language stimulation in their most fluent language. This will serve as a supportive base for parent-child relationships as well as linguistic input of highest possible quantity and quality. As soon as possible, the family must be assisted to develop competency in use of those transmission modes that are selected by mutual agreement of family and educational agency as most effective for the child.

Parents who speak a native language other than English should be aided in acquiring the second-language fluency and cultural familiarity they will need to assist the child in early acquisition of the second-language system. In the Netherlands, there are a number of guest workers from such countries as Turkey, Spain, Portugal, and Indonesia whose native language is not Dutch. Their deaf children are expected to acquire Dutch in the special schools for the hearing impaired. There is no special bilingual consideration. The assumption is that both children and parents must learn the language of the majority as rapidly as possible (Kopp, 1981). Presently, the number of such children appears to be small. It is difficult to predict what might occur if the proportion of minority in-migrants should increase. It may be that the historic European expectancy of true bilingual competency will continue to prevail (as was true in the United States in the first half of this century) and that children, hearing or deaf, will be expected to acquire the majority language in school as promptly as possible.

Assessment

In order to provide early, appropriate, systematic intervention for deaf children of bilingual parents, linguistic and phonologic competencies must be assessed with instruments that can differentiate between bilingual influences, transmission problems, and functional or organic disorders. A period of clinical, diagnostic teaching that combines individual and small peer-group activities provides an appropriate physical and emotional setting in which a team of experienced diagnostic clinicians and teachers may explore the child's functional competencies. It is important that the family be considered as part of the team and share in the interpretation of results, choice of strategies for evaluation and teaching, selection of transmission modes, and development of short- and long-term goals. Experienced interpreters and diagnosticians fluent in the appropriate Hispanic dialect and knowledgeable about the ethnic/cultural values must be included on the team. Thus, if the parents are Hispanic and deaf, at least one team member must be fluent in the relevant transmission modes and one in the native language. Ideally, all team members would be fluent bilinguals able to communicate in all modes.

Although the use of standard test instruments may be of value for research data, there are particular advantages in the evaluation of spontaneous or situationally elicited, context-dependent language. Language generally is learned for social reasons (Ervin-Tripp, 1973), and performance competency is manifested by those functionally bilingual individuals who are able to manipulate conceptual language with facile control of the input/output symbol codes and systems used in transmitting two languages. It is somewhat more difficult to assess input competency and storage strategies in the early stages of language acquisition, particularly if output transmission modes are relatively dysfluent. Too frequently in such cases, the diagnostician resorts to scorable tests of labeling as a substitute for examination of the more complex interface of the individual's conceptual system and the syntactic and semantic systems of the target language (Nelson, 1981). It is essential that the clinician discriminate between superficial fluency in the target language and fluency that permits conceptual development and cognitive processing. The choice of culturally relevant assessment contexts, situations, test items, materials, and strategies may have significant effect on the results. Awareness of culturally linked behavioral patterns such as avoidance of eye contact with authority figures or the preference for minimal, direct physical contact, may prevent skewing of the results and help to elicit maximal effort. An assessment/intervention model of cognitive processing (Kopp, 1968) provides a basis for the systematic selection of input, classification, storage, retrieval, and output functions to be assessed. Since there is general agreement that, in normal acquisition of language, input precedes output, such a model also serves as a progressive, sequential framework for the specification of intervention strategies appropriate to development of requisite competencies.

Intervention

Ideally, early intervention will permit the optimal development of true bilingualism in deaf children. Lambert asserts that, compared with late bilinguals, early bilinguals process deep meaning better in both languages (Lambert, 1969; Lambert & Rawlings, 1969; Lambert, 1981). Although the argument has not been resolved in favor of either sequential or simultaneous bilingual acquisition, Cummins' language interdependence hypothesis supports the belief that proficiency in a second language is dependent on literacy related functions of the previous language (Cummins, 1980). Thus, the threshold theory for second language acquisition appears to predict the possibility of cognitive processing deficits if the child has not developed cognitive competency in one language before the second is initiated. After conceptual language is at threshold, the second language can be added. American Sign Language is generally accepted as a unique and separate language (Bellugi & Studdert-Kennedy, in press), meeting the conceptual requirement for a primary language. However, it does not include the graphic reading and writing or the oral/aural transmission modes common to majority languages.

References

Albert, M., & Obler, L. *The bilingual brain.* New York: Academic Press, 1978.

Bellugi, U. *Annual Report, Salk Institute Laboratory for Language and Cognitive Studies.* Unpublished report, Salk Institute, 1980.

Bellugi, U., & Studdert-Kennedy, M. (Eds.). *Signed and spoken language: Biological constraints on linguistic form.* Basel: Verlag Chemie, in press.

Ben Zeev, S. *The influence of bilingualism on cognitive development and cognitive strategy.* Unpublished doctoral dissertation, University of Chicago, 1972.

Cummins, J. *The construct of language proficiency in bilingual education.* Paper presented at Georgetown Round Table on Languages and Linguistics, Washington, D.C., 1980.

Ervin-Tripp, S. *Language acquisition and communicative choice.* Stanford: Stanford University Press, 1973.

Kopp, H. Curriculum as a process. In H. Kopp (Ed.), *Curriculum, cognition, and content.* Washington, D.C.: Alexander Graham Bell Association for the Deaf, 1968. (Monograph)

Kopp, H. Oral education redefined. In A. Mulholland (Ed.), *Oral education today and tomorrow.* Washington, D.C.: Alexander Graham Bell Association for the Deaf, 1981.

Kopp, H. Bilingual problems: Mexican-Americans, American-Indians. In *Proceedings of the International Congress on Education of the Deaf,* Hamburg, West Germany, August 4–8, 1980 (Vol. 2). Heidelberg: J. Groos Verlag, 1982.

Lambert, W. Psychological studies of the interdependencies of the bilingual's two languages. In J. Pulvel (Ed.), *Substance and structure of language.* Los Angeles: University of California Press, 1969.

Lambert, W. Bilingualism and language acquisition. In H. Winitz (Ed.), Native language and foreign language acquisition. *Annals of the New York Academy of Sciences,* 1981, 379, 9–22.

Lambert, W., & Rawlings, C. Bilingual processing of mixed language associative networks. *Journal of Verbal Learning and Verbal Behavior,* 8, 604–609.

Nelson, K. Acquisition of words by first-language learners. In H. Winitz (Ed.), Native language and foreign language acquisition. *Annals of the New York Academy of Sciences,* 1981, 379, 148–159.

Obler, L., Zatorre, R., Galloway, L., & Vaid, J. Cerebral lateralization in bilinguals: Methodological issues. *Brain and Language,* 1982, *15,* 40–54.

Ojemann, G., & Whitaker, H. Language localization and variability. *Brain and Language,* 1978, *6,* 239–260.

Sussman, H., Franklin, P., & Simon, T. Bilingual speech: Bilateral control? *Brain and Language,* 1982, *15,* 125–142.

Vaid, J., & Lambert, W. Differential cerebral involvement in the cognitive functioning of bilinguals. *Brain and Language,* 1979, *8,* 92–110.

The Language Choices

7

The Language of Instruction for Hearing-Impaired Students from Non-English-Speaking Homes: A Framework for Considering Alternatives

Walter G. Secada

Hearing-impaired students from non-English-speaking homes represent a special challenge for educators. The educators not only must think in the specialized terms common for educating special populations; they also must break beyond those terms to include the perspectives from other specialty areas with which they have had little (if any) contact. For instance, some years ago a school specializing in educating the deaf was confronted with a profoundly deaf girl from a Hispanic home who, in the words of one staff member, "spoke nothing but gibberish." Sometime later, an alert teacher realized that the girl was speaking Spanish, badly articulated, but understandable to her family. The child's educational program had to be revamped to take account of her newly discovered abilities: lipreading (in Spanish), speech, and a somewhat developed vocabulary.

Alternately, on more than one occasion I have spoken with a bilingual, ESL, or mainstream teacher who has noticed that a particular student is having difficulty learning English or following the coursework, even though instruction may be in that student's native language. Some of these teachers, particularly those in regular classrooms, assume that such students are having difficulty because their native language is weak or is interfering with learning English. Further discussion with these teachers usually reveals that these students have not been tested for possible hearing loss. In sum, there

This paper is based on work done in preparation for workshops supported by the Office of Bilingual Education and Minority Languages Affairs, U.S. Department of Education, under Grant #G008200708. Any opinions, findings, conclusions, and recommendations expressed are the author's and do not necessarily reflect the views of either OBEMLA or ED.

seems to be a myopia on the part of some specialists; they tend to cast problems only in terms of their specialization, failing to recognize when they must go beyond that specialization and test alternatives.

Furthermore, an educator who correctly identifies a student as being hearing impaired and having a non-English language background is then confronted with a vast array of language options, together with reasons for choosing any of them, in selecting a program for the student's education. Someone who believes that such a student will have great difficulty learning even one language (and that this language should be that of the larger society) might choose a program model that stresses the learning of oral English skills. Recent research on sign language might lead another person to opt for a total communication model which mixes oral language (usually English) with sign in an effort to maximize the language input of the student.*

Alternately, someone wishing to maintain the student's family ties—and possibly to exploit what oral native language the student already has developed—might opt for an oral bilingual approach incorporating (modified) English as a second language (ESL) techniques (e.g., Bolen, 1981). Finally, a multilingual approach might seem appealing to someone wishing to strengthen the student's native language skills while simultaneously teaching sign language and English oral skills (e.g., Fischgrund, 1982a).

There is little research to guide us in choosing from among these and other options. Therefore, educators must rely on reasons such as those just given and on the experiences of others who have chosen language options for educating similar students. However, such experiences and perspectives can be myopic because they are often based on a single point of view: the student is seen as "just" hearing impaired or "only" from a non-English background and hence "only" limited English proficient (LEP). The purpose of this chapter is to address that problem by presenting a framework for describing various language options for educating hearing-impaired students from non-English-speaking homes.

---

*The term *total communication* has been broadly defined by CEASC as "a philosophy incorporating appropriate aural, manual, and oral modes of communication in order to ensure effective communication with and among hearing-impaired persons" (quoted in Garretson, 1976, p.91). When referring to the generic and broad phenomenon—including all cases of dual sign/oral productions—the term *total communication* will be used in this paper, in keeping with that broad definition. When referring to the more narrow form of total communication in which a one-to-one morphemic match between oral and sign systems is attempted, the term *exact English* will be used to represent the various systems that make such an attempt.

This framework is based on the major language options for educating LEP students and for educating hearing-impaired students. The framework in Table 1 was derived by crossing these two sets of options. This system provides a first step in organizing the myriad options from a perspective that combines two specializations, bilingual and deaf education. In the following section, the major features of that framework and some of its implications for staff and program development will be presented. In the section after that, we will consider how individual differences and cultural considerations might lead to the choice of particular options. In the last section of this chapter, some directions for further development of this framework will be discussed.

The Framework

The (vertical) columns in Table 1 are headed by the three major language options for LEP students: use of English only; use of two languages, English and the student's first (native or home) language; and exclusive use of the student's native language. The (horizontal) rows cover the major language modality options for the education of a hearing-impaired student: exclusive use of the oral mode, a mixture of oral and manual (i.e., speech and signs together), and the exclusive use of the manual mode (i.e., signs).

The major headings should serve two functions. First, they should be construed broadly to incorporate a variety of options under each principal category. Second, they should serve as reminders about the various staffing and programmatic commitments that are implied by choosing to implement a particular program. The major headings will be discussed first, then the derived categories.

Language Options for LEP Students

For the normal LEP student the first option, sole reliance on English, includes two subcategories. One is to allow the student to sink or swim in an all-English educational setting; this practice was declared unconstitutional by the Supreme Court in *Lau v. Nichols* (1974; see also Leibowitz, 1982). The other is to provide the student with special training in English as a second language (ESL) so that, while attending classes, the student is taught how to speak and to understand English. Typically, ESL classes are taught by specialists who coordinate their instruction to what is being taught in the student's regular classes (Celce-Murcia & McIntosh, 1979; Paulston & Bruder, 1976).

Table 1
Language/Modality Options for Hearing-Impaired Students
from Non-English-Speaking Homes

Modality Options for Hearing-Impaired Students	Language Options for Limited-English-Proficient (LEP) Students		
	English	English and Native Language	Native Language
Oral	1 English as a second language (ESL)	2 Bilingual education	3 Oral native language
Oral and Manual	4 Rochester Method, Total communication, Exact English	5 (Projecto Oportunidad)	6 Oral/manual native language mixtures
Manual	7 American Sign Language (ASL), Pidgin sign	8 ASL & native country sign language	9 Native country sign language

The second major language option for LEP students includes a variety of programs, all under the rubric of bilingual education. These programs are characterized by the use of both the student's native (home) language and English as media of instruction. Program models typically vary according to when and how each language is used. Sometimes, the two languages are used separately; one language is used for some courses (or at particular times of the day, or in particular parts of the room) and the other language is used for the balance of the coursework. Alternately, both languages might be mixed freely within the student's courses (Seelye & Navarro, 1977).

Depending on how English and the native language are mixed in the program, different staffing patterns could be used. Teacher aides might provide individual assistance for students in a regular classroom; or a certified bilingual teacher who speaks the students' native language might teach specific content at specific times using specialized methods and native language materials (see Cohen, 1980; Hernandez, 1976; Office of Bilingual Education, 1981). Bilingual programs for LEP students usually incorporate ESL in their instructional designs.

The third option for LEP students is exclusive use of the students' native language. Though very uncommon in public schools, this option can be exercised by students attending private schools. Public schools might offer this option to recently arrived immigrant students while they become acclimated to the U.S. educational system. For example, the Dade County (Miami) school system opened a series of special schools to serve the large influx of Cuban refugee students who entered Florida with the Mariel exodus during 1979–80. Until these students were ready to enter the school system's regular bilingual programs, all of their initial schooling was in Spanish.

Modality Options for Hearing-Impaired Students

For a hearing-impaired student, the language options relate to the channels of language production: mouth (oral modality), hands (manual modality), or a combination of oral and manual modalities. The oral modality—what Schlesinger (1978) calls "spoken English"—involves the development of oral language skills: use of residual hearing with the assistance of hearing aids and the development of lipreading skills and speech production. An audiologist tests each student for degree of hearing loss, recommends appropriate hearing aids, and teaches the student to develop any residual hearing. Speech and language pathologists provide speech training. Bradford and Hardy (1979), Davis and Silverman (1978), and Moores (1982) offer more detailed descriptions of the oral modality. A seldom used oral-only option—the auditory method—concentrates exclusively on the development of listening skills. Reading and writing are discouraged until children have developed some oral skills; lipreading is not taught (Moores, 1982).

The second option, combined oral and manual modalities, is what Schlesinger (1978) calls "visual English." It involves three approaches. The first is the simultaneous production of speech and fingerspelling, known as the Rochester Method. This fingerspelling involves manually spelling each word, as it is spoken, using 26 configurations of the hands that represent the letters of the alphabet. A series of hand configurations can thus represent a word. The second approach is the simultaneous production of speech and a mixture of signs and fingerspelling. The sign production roughly corresponds to the oral (English) production. The signs are supplemented by fingerspelling of prefixes, suffixes, and other markers in an effort to obtain a one-to-one match between the morphemes in speech and in sign. In this paper the second method is labeled *exact English*. The manual production parallels speech and therefore maintains English syntax. Educational programs involving either of these approaches will typically incorporate other features from oral programs such as lipreading and the use of residual hearing. The third approach, total communication, encourages development of all these communication modes, as appropriate. Certified teachers of the deaf would know and understand total communication as well as special instructional methods and materials for use within the classroom (Moores, 1982). The third approach here involves a less strict match between the oral and sign modalities and covers a wide range. Syntax may follow English, American Sign Language (ASL), or a mixture of the two. Morphemes, words, or higher linguistic units may be found in one production stream and be omitted from the other.

The third major option is the exclusive use of the manual modality. Exclusive use of the manual modality could also be the use of a language other than English; in the U.S. that is American Sign Language (ASL). As the native language of the deaf in this country, ASL is a real language with its own rules for grammar and syntax, this is described in greater detail in Klima and Bellugi (1979) and Wilbur (1979). Exclusive use of ASL is rare in deaf education. Other forms of signing are possible under this option. These forms have developed from the mixing of English and ASL. Bornstein (1978) called these systems "pidgin sign." The exclusive reliance on signing (i.e., the manual modality) most likely would occur in individual classes in which the teacher had a high level of fluency in ASL.

The first and second options—oral and combined oral/manual—represent the most commonly followed practices for educating the deaf in the United States. Just as there is great variation even within language options for education of LEP students, so is there much variation within language modalities for education of the hearing impaired. Programs might agree on modality yet consciously stress different facets. Furthermore, actual practices within a school might vary to such an extent that the approach used is consistent in name only. For example, informal observation in schools for the deaf leads me to conclude that the strict use of exact English (i.e., of there being a precise one-to-one match between oral and manual morphemic productions) is very rare. More commonly, teachers omit endings, functors, and entire words in their signing; students often use signs without either following English syntax or using extensive speech.

Despite the variation within each option, these categories represent the major programmatic options for educating hearing-impaired students. We now turn to the framework which results from crossing these options with the options for educating LEP students.

Locating Programmatic Options

The criteria for locating a programmatic option in Table 1 concerns a mixture of the modality, educational uses, and literacy goals of the language of instruction. For example, the use of English within an ESL program is geared to the use and development of English literacy (i.e., reading and writing) skills. If the student's native language is used, materials in that language are usually a part of the curriculum. Thus some literacy in the student's native language is either presupposed or is developed in most bilingual approaches. These criteria lead to the placement of the language options for LEP students across the first row (oral modality) of Table 1.

The placement of the modality options for hearing-impaired students, similarly, is down the first column (English) of Table 1. The status of American Sign Language within the framework is open to some interpretation. On the one hand, it is an independent language serving as the native or home language for a sizable number of hearing-impaired students; thus one might argue that it has the same status as a "foreign" or non-English home language and should be placed in Block 9. From an educational point of view, however, a crucial distinction should be made regarding the development of literacy and academic skills. No educational program based on ASL uses or develops literacy skills in a language other than English. Unlike the case for other languages such as Native American languages, which at one time lacked orthographies, there has been no attempt to develop a written version for ASL. Thus, ASL supports the development and use of English literacy skills, while another sign language would support a different set of literacy skills. Based on this educational distinction, ASL belongs in Block 7.

The location of these major options along either the first row (Blocks 1,2,3) or the the first column (Blocks 1,4,7) graphically illustrates the problem of myopia described above. Moreover, gaps in the original program designs and staffing patterns become obvious. Programs from the LEP axis in the first row acquire an oralist flavor indicating that, at the very least, these programs should incorporate the concerns of those involved in developing oral skills among hearing-impaired students. Program staff would need to add audiologists and speech and hearing pathologists to their regular staff to provide input and expertise. Similarly, programs from the hearing-impaired axis take on the flavor of an English language option for LEP students. Thus the perspectives from this category should be included in modifying the program's design. One requirement is for ESL teachers and counselors to understand cultural issues in serving LEP students. Finally, the dual perspective of the derived framework provides four more options (Table 1, Blocks 5,6,8 and 9) than would arise from simply combining the individual points of view from each specialty.

Coordination of Responsibilities

In taking this broader view, program planners must take care to coordinate staff qualifications and responsibilities. For example, an oral program might follow a modified bilingual approach (Block 2) such as that recommended by Bolen (1981) for students with "mild, moderate, or moderate-to-severe hearing loss." This would require coordinating the responsibilities of the bilingual and ESL teachers from the bilingual component and the responsibilities of the audiologists and speech instructors from the hearing-impaired component. These responsibilities need not fall upon four different individuals; however, care must be taken to ensure that the perspectives represented by each task are fully articulated and coordinated with respect to the other tasks. For instance, the bilingual teacher should be sure that students can lipread and understand words and phrases used in their home language. For this, the teacher should consult with audiologists and speech pathologists, borrowing their methods and ensuring that their efforts are reinforced during instruction. Similarly, audiologists might incorporate exercises from the student's native-language classroom into their own work with the student. Hybrid programs such as this require that staff receive training on the perspectives of the the methods used by other staff. Otherwise, confusion, gaps in the student's education, and general chaos will result.

For students demonstrating an oral language dominance in Portuguese or Spanish, the Rhode Island School for the Deaf offers a program combining oral instruction in that student's dominant (i.e., native) language, modified instruction in English as a second language, and instruction via total communication in English and sign (Fischgrund, 1982b). This program (Block 5) combines features of bilingual education (native-language instruction and ESL) with features of total communication.

The purposes of Projecto Oportunidad (as this program is known) are many. Content coursework such as mathematics is conducted in spoken Portuguese or spoken Spanish. This serves to strengthen the student's home language (often the only language spoken by his or her parents); it also exploits whatever language or cognitive development may have occurred prior to entering school (such as lipreading, ability to count, or the use of residual hearing). English as a second language is taught in an effort to enhance the transfer of oral skills from the student's native language to English. For example, a student who has learned to lipread Spanish can then learn to lipread English, provided care is taken to minimize confusion between the languages. Finally, total communication is used when mainstreaming the student. Staffing includes bilingual teachers, fluent in Spanish or Portuguese, who coordinate their work with audiologists, speech pathologists, and special teachers for the deaf. Furthermore, paraprofessionals who are fluent in the students' home languages serve as liaisons between the school and parents. According to this model, staffing for an individualized education plan (IEP) meeting could include translators for the parents as well as for the student.

Other programs can be designed similarly. A native-language program stressing oral skills (Table 1, Block 3) would require classroom teachers, fluent in the student's native language, who would coordinate their teaching with the work being done by the audiologists and other staff specializing in hearing impairment. Within such a program, primary leadership might fall upon the native-language teacher, who would have the most direct contact with the student. A native-language program stressing oral and manual communication development (Block 6) would require teachers who know the students' native languages. Similarly, a native-country sign language program (Block 9) would require coordinated services between teachers who could use the sign language of the student's country and those who could not.

Obviously the feasibility of various program options will depend on staff availability and resource allocation. However no option should be dismissed out of hand; there are occasions in which the more esoteric option is more appropriate. Some of these occasions will be presented in the next section.

Choosing an Option

As noted, the belief that students cannot handle learning more than one language might lead a program planner to recommend an English oral program (Block 1). The reasons against such a naive approach can be found in the literature from both bilingual and deaf education. However, it is very possible for the student to choose this option. A recent Israeli immigrant, fluent in Israeli Sign Language and steadily learning ASL, insisted on learning to read English by first learning to speak it (Mayberry, 1981). For such a student, English as a second language would be indicated.

Indochinese refugee students may have suffered hearing losses arising from untreated ear infections or other traumas suffered while in refugee camps in Southeast Asia. These students' native language oral skills should be relatively advanced; however, their learning of English will probably prove to be long and tedious unless we first exploit and develop the oral skills they already have. Lipreading and use of residual hearing should be developed first in the students' home language through an oralist native-language program (Block 3). Education in English, exact English, or total communication probably should be delayed until progress is made in those receptive native-language skills.

For individuals with oral English skills (e.g., hearing people), sign language is initially taught by relating signs to their spoken counterparts. For the student with oral skills in another language, initial instruction in sign language might follow a similar format, except that signs would be related to their counterparts in the student's native language. Needless to say, this strategy would require the close cooperation of the native-language and sign-language teachers. Finally, either exact English or total communication—building on the student's native language as well as any sign language or (modified) ESL skills—might be used to develop the student's oral English skills. Thus, for a student who suffers a hearing loss later in life, second (sign) and third (English) language development would build upon his or her native language.

A second reason for developing the hearing-impaired student's home language through a multilingual model (Blocks 2, 3, 5, or 6 for students with hearing parents; Blocks 8 or 9 for those with deaf parents who sign) involves the student's family and the ethnic community. Programs that develop English oral or sign skills to the exclusion of the student's home language risk confusing and alienating the student from family and community. Consider a Hispanic student attempting to lipread Spanish using skills developed for English; or, consider the family's confusion in trying to understand the student's signed English when Spanish is the language at home. Concern in this regard has been expressed by Mexican-American parents of hearing-impaired students who feel that their children's educators "often disregard parental goals of bilingual/bicultural education...and create an unnecessary language barrier between parent and child" (Luetke, 1976, pp. 566–567). One solution to this problem is to include native-language instruction in the student's program, as is done by the Rhode Island School for the

Deaf. A complementary solution would be to provide ESL and/or sign language instruction to the student's family. Initial sign language instruction would probably be adapted by relating signs to their counterparts in the parent's native language.

Hearing-impaired students immigrating from countries where oralism has been very strong (Germany, Great Britain, Portugal, France) might prefer and do better in programs with a strong oral flavor (Blocks 1, 2, and 3). These students should have the option of bilingual education (Block 2) so that, while they learn English, their education does not progressively fall behind that of their peers.

On the other hand, students arriving from countries in which the use of sign language is not discouraged (Sweden, Denmark, Poland) could prosper in schools using total communication (Blocks 4, 5, and 6). There are many sign languages throughout the world, and we do not know how easy or difficult it might be to learn ASL based on prior knowledge of another sign language. Thus, students who are placed in simultaneous communication environments will probably need time to adapt and to learn the new languages. For these students, bilingual/bimodal education (Block 5) using total communication in their native language should be the initial option.

Non-oral students will probably prove quite resistant to learning oral English skills, preferring to learn American Sign Language (or a pidgin variant) and to transfer their academic skills via ASL. Some form of bilingual education employing ASL and the students' native language (Block 8) would be indicated for these students.

As the above examples illustrate, reasons for choosing one program option over another will vary from case to case. Before ruling out an option that seems impractical, the program planner should conduct a careful review of school and community resources to see if a variant of that option can be implemented. For example, if a student knows a native sign language, someone from the student's family might also. If that person can assist in the student's education as an aide or tutor, a bridge can be created between the student's native language and new experiences.

In planning for either the LEP student or for the hearing-impaired student, educators too often base their decisions on what the students are missing—English skills, hearing, oral language, manual skills, or academic development. What also needs to be considered, and what is stressed in the above examples, is knowledge and ability that the student already possesses. If educational programs build on the student's abilities, they should have an easier time coping with the student's deficits. An initial description of the student's abilities should include not only linguistic abilities (see chapter 9) and prior academic background, but also familial and cultural background (see chapter 5). Considering all of these factors and the interplay among them leads to a more informed decision about which language system should be used in that student's education. This decision should be revised periodically in light of new information about the student's abilities and progress.

Future Work

The above framework is meant to help educators systematize the decisions they must make when choosing the language(s) that will be used in educating hearing-impaired students from non-English-speaking homes. The above scenarios illustrate some conditions under which one (or more) language program designs might be followed; the descriptions of each program's components suggested the staff responsibilities and coordination needed to implement that program.

Future work on these categories will need to proceed in three directions. First, the framework itself needs testing to see if the categories help guide decisions about language use. With so many options, and so many considerations prior to choosing a program model, the test will be how well this framework facilitates appropriate language choices and mixes. This testing may also suggest improvements in the framework.

Second, greater attention must be paid to planning curriculum and instruction for this twice special population. As Moores (1982) points out, the average deaf student leaves school reading below fifth-grade level and doing mathematics below sixth-grade level. For the student from a non-English-speaking home, the picture is probably bleaker. How to adapt curriculum and specialized instructional strategies from deaf and bilingual education to appropriate language options is no trivial task.

Third, research is needed on a wide variety of special education issues and methodologies. These range from in-depth case studies concerning the how and why of certain decisions to more formal longitudinal assessments of student progress which might test the validity of those decisions. Because current educational research priorities do not include the populations considered here, other methods of generating knowledge about the education of hearing-impaired students from non-English-speaking homes will need to be developed. This includes forming networks among like-minded educators who will approach questions in a flexible, pragmatic manner—trying things out, keeping what works, and abandoning what fails.

Anyone familiar with the 400-year-old oral versus manual debate within deaf education—or the more recent English-only versus native-language debate in bilingual education—can appreciate how difficult it is to admit that we honestly do not know the best way to proceed. In this case, the proper question is, Under what conditions should particular language(s) be used in educating a specific kind of hearing-impaired student from a specific kind of non-English-speaking home? We know that no single option seems best for all students given their diverse backgrounds. The framework presented here is a first attempt to conceptualize the various options open to these diverse people.

References

Bolen, D. Issues relating to language choice: Hearing-impaired infants from bilingual homes. *Volta Review*, 1981, *83*(6), 410–412.

Bornstein, H. Sign language in the education of the deaf. In I. M. Schlesinger & L. Namir (Eds.), *Sign language of the deaf: Psychological, linguistic, and sociological perspectives*. New York: Academic Press, 1978.

Bradford, L., & Hardy, W. (Eds.). *Hearing and hearing impairment*. New York: Grune & Stratton, 1979.

Celce-Murcia, M., & McIntosh, L. (Eds.). *Teaching English as a second or foreign language*. Rowley, Mass.: Newbury House, 1979.

Cohen, A. D. *Describing bilingual education classrooms: The role of the teacher in evaluation*. Rosslyn, Va.: National Clearinghouse for Bilingual Education, 1980.

Davis, H., & Silverman, S. R. (Eds.). *Hearing and deafness* (4th ed.). New York: Holt, Rinehart & Winston, 1978.

Delgado, G. L. Hearing-impaired children from non-native language homes. *American Annals of the Deaf*, 1981, *126*, 118–121. An adaptation of this article may be found on pages 28–36.

Fischgrund, J. E. Language intervention for hearing-impaired children from linguistically and culturally diverse backgrounds. *Topics in Language Disorders*, 1982, *2*(3), 57–66. (a) An adaptation of this article may be found on pages 94–104.

Fischgrund, J. E. Personal communication, April 1982. (b)

Garretson, M. D. Total communication. In R. D. Frisina (Ed.), *A bicentennial monograph on hearing impairment: Trends in the U.S.A.* Washington, D.C.: A. G. Bell Association for the Deaf, 1976.

Hernandez, L. *Training manual for bilingual bicultural education teachers.* Grand Rapids, Mich.: Grand Valley State College, 1976.

Klima, E., & Bellugi, U. *The signs of language.* Cambridge, Mass.: Harvard University Press, 1979.

Lau v. Nichols, 414 U.S. 563 (1974).

Leibowitz, A.H. *Federal recognition of the rights of language minority groups.* Rosslyn, Va.: National Clearinghouse for Bilingual Education, 1982.

Luetke, B. Questionnaire results from Mexican-American parents of hearing-impaired children in the United States. *American Annals of the Deaf*, 1976, *121*, 565–568.

Mayberry, R. Personal communication, May 1981.

Moores, D. A. *Educating the deaf: Psychology, principles, and practices* (2nd ed.). Boston: Houghton Mifflin, 1982.

Office of Bilingual Bicultural Education, Department of Education, California. *Schooling and language minority students: A theoretical framework.* Los Angeles: Evaluation, Dissemination, and Assessment Center, California Department of Education, 1981.

Paulston, C. B., & Bruder, M. N. *Teaching English as a second language: Techniques and procedures.* Cambridge, Mass.: Winthrop, 1976.

Schlesinger, H. S. The acquisition of bimodal language. In I. M. Schlesinger & L. Namir (Eds.), *Sign language of the deaf: Psychological, linguistic, and sociological perspectives.* New York: Academic Press, 1978.

Seelye, H. N., & Navarro, B. N. *A guide to the selection of bilingual education program designs.* Arlington Heights, Ill.: Bilingual Education Service Center, 1977.

Wilbur, R. *American Sign Language and language systems.* Baltimore: University Park Press, 1979.

8

Language Intervention for Hearing-Impaired Children from Linguistically and Culturally Diverse Backgrounds

Joseph E. Fischgrund

The principal of the Rhode Island School for the Deaf received an inquiry in 1921 from a Brown University professor of social sciences inquiring about the children of foreign born families who attended the school for the deaf. The principal replied that more than half of the school children had immigrant parents who did not speak English. "In the families of foreign parentage I find the progress in speech and language much retarded," he said, noting that even if the parents spoke English, "it is 'broken English,' hard to interpret by people with all their faculties, and particularly puzzling for a speech or lip reader" (Hurd, 1921).

Unfortunately, the observation that deaf children from non-English-speaking homes face additional difficulties in school was to go virtually unnoticed in deaf education for more than half a century. Responding to the increasing number of Hispanic students in programs for the hearing impaired in New York City, Lerman and Cortez (1977) conducted an extensive survey of hearing-impaired students in that area. They noted that "a disproportionate number [of Hispanic students] are placed in the low achieving or learning disabled groups in the schools" (p. 1). Lerman also cited data from Jensema (1975) that "Spanish-American deaf students have lower achievement levels than white deaf students and, in vocabulary and reading comprehension, lower levels than other minority groups surveyed" (p. 10).

National awareness began to grow concerning the difficulties that hearing-impaired students from non-English-speaking (NES) homes were encountering in school. Delgado (see chapter 3) conducted the first thorough national study of hearing-impaired students from NES homes. The number of these students nationally was reflective of the overall population of Hispanics and other NES groups, but the placement of students within programs for the hearing impaired was dramatically different. Whereas 29 percent of all students in programs for the hearing impaired reportedly had handicapping conditions in addition to hearing impairment, 51 percent of the students from NES homes were described as having additional handicapping conditions. In the categories of mental retardation, emotional or behavioral disorder, and specific learning disability, the incidence of additional disabilities among hearing-impaired students from NES homes was three to four times larger than for students in the general hearing-impaired population.

Responding to changes in its own population, the Rhode Island School for the Deaf initiated bilingual/bicultural services in 1975. The program has resulted in lower dropout rates, better attendance, increased parent participation, and, in a surprising side effect, a greater degree of mainstreaming for students from NES homes. In developing such a program, it is important to address the complex linguistic, sociolinguistic, and cultural issues inherent in developing a bilingual/bicultural program for linguistically and culturally diverse hearing-impaired children.

Linguistic Considerations

Because it is so hard for the deaf child to learn one language, how can we burden the child with the task of learning two languages? This is the most immediate response to bilingual programming for hearing-impaired students. The response is unwarranted for several reasons, most of which center around the conditions under which first and second languages are acquired.

First, the hearing-impaired child does not have a choice when it comes to the oral language environment of his or her home. Because exposure to language is the first step in language development, hearing-impaired children entering educational programs, no matter how severe their hearing loss, have already begun the process of language acquisition. This position rejects the notion that such children have no language and accepts the view that language is more than just an inventory of producible phonemes or testable vocabulary (e.g., Halliday, 1974). Whatever the language competence of the child, even if on a preverbal level, the child is acquiring the language of the home. Obviously, the child acquires only that language to which he or she is exposed.

Bolen (1981) suggests that "if the child has a severe-to-profound hearing loss...from a linguistic point of view the educational process would be facilitated if the child were exposed to only one language" (p. 411). What Bolen fails to account for here is that the child has already been exposed to one language and will continue to be exposed to that language as long as it is the language of the home. Contrary to Bolen's position, my contention is that this early exposure to the home language must be accounted for in the child's early educational program, and that his or her continued exposure to the home language must be taken into account throughout the child's educational career.

Many hearing-impaired students, especially those with less than profound losses, do have demonstrable abilities in their native language when they enter the U.S. (mainland) educational system. This range of abilities needs to be assessed along two parameters: the level of ability in the first language and the degree of bilingualism, if any. The nature of linguistic abilities along these two parameters is probably the critical factor in educational success for children entering school with significant degrees of residual hearing. As Bolen (1981) notes: "If the child has a mild, moderate, or moderate-to-severe hearing loss, there appears to be no reason why he or she cannot be bilingual from the start" (p. 411).

Historically, programs for hearing-impaired students from NES homes have been designed for their hearing impairment but not for their underlying language abilities. For example, the moderately hearing-impaired adolescent with demonstrable proficiency in Spanish will generally be placed with students of his or her age level who have the lowest degree of English functioning or in a life skills or other program for low-functioning deaf students. If the program is in a school for the deaf, the student most likely will be placed with students having a far greater degree of hearing loss or with students whose problems in the acquisition of English are different. For example, in their study of New York City schools for the deaf, Lerman and Cortez (1977) found significant differences in the age of onset category, "where 30 percent of all Hispanic students are reported as becoming deaf after birth, compared to 22 percent of the 'white' population" (p. 3).

For hearing-impaired students from NES homes to have equal access to the specially designed services available to other hearing-impaired individuals, they need to have access to the language of that education—English. Conversely, programs for the hearing impaired need to adapt to the language abilities of the students as they enter the program. If there are educationally adequate abilities in the first language, then educational progress can continue in the home language while English is being acquired as a second language. For the hearing-impaired child whose language abilities are delayed in the first language because of the presence of the impairment, the optimal conditions under which the child will begin to enter into a second language-learning process includes continued development and use of the first language.

Support for this approach (for both hearing and hearing-impaired children) is found in the developmental interdependence hypothesis (Cummins, 1979). This hypothesis proposes that "the level of L2 [the second language] competence which a bilingual child attains is partially a function of the type of competence the child has developed in L1 [the first language] at the time when intensive exposure to L2 begins" (p. 222). Without attention to this linguistic interdependence, most hearing-impaired children find themselves in the situation described by Cummins: "If in an early stage of development a minority child finds itself in a foreign-language learning environment without contemporaneously receiving the requisite support in its mother tongue, the development of its skill in the mother tongue will slow down and even cease, leaving the child without a basis for learning the second language" (p. 233).

This situation, the most common one for most hearing-impaired children at all levels of hearing loss, explains the two most common complaints about hearing-impaired children from NES homes: complaints from the parents that the child is losing his or her home language and complaints from the teacher that the child is not doing well in school. Rather than explain these difficulties by saying, in the first case, that the child would rather speak English or, in the second case, that the child has an additional disability, one only has to look to the developmental interdependence hypothesis to understand why communication breakdown in the home and poor academic achievement are interrelated.

A Crucial Principle

Acquiring a language and learning through language are two very different tasks. In order for the second even to become a possibility, the first—the process of language acquisition—must not only be happening but must have reached a certain threshold level. According to Cummins (1979), "there may be threshold levels of linguistic competence which a bilingual child must attain both in order to avoid cognitive disadvantages and allow the potentially beneficial aspects of bilingualism to influence his or her cognitive and academic functioning" (p. 222). Consider a child who has greater competence in the home language but who is asked to learn in English. Cummins' hypothesis would predict that the child will not only suffer a cognitive disadvantage in the learning process but also that whatever potential benefits are to be had from the child's abilities in his or her first language will be dissipated. For the child who has a hearing impairment this principle, which involves the central role that language plays in the educational process, is of utmost importance in explaining the difficulties hearing-impaired children from NES homes have experienced to date. The principle is crucial in developing language and educational programs that utilize all of the student's language abilities and that do not place him or her at a cognitive disadvantage relative to hearing-impaired peers.

This mismatch between home and school languages involves more than the fact that the language at school is English and the language at home is other than English. The function of language in school and the form that it takes are very unlike the form and function of language in the home. As Halliday (1974) notes: "The child who does not succeed in the school system may be one who is not using language in the ways required by the school; the failure of a student to master school skills is part of a more general problem—the fundamental mismatch between the child's linguistic capabilities and the demands that are made upon them" (p. 18). The mismatch is more than just a consequence of school and home languages having different surface structures; it is a mismatch between the ways languages are used at home and the way language is used in school. Halliday focuses on three areas of language functioning—the interpersonal (with properties arising from its use in social interaction), the ideational (which involves the use of language in conceptual learning), and the textual (with properties arising from the structure of the language itself), and points to aspects of the ideational area as "crucial to success in school" (p. 18).

For children from NES homes, this mismatch between the function of language at home and at school can be described in terms of the language being either context-embedded or context-reduced (Cummins, 1981). According to Cummins, "context-embedded communication is more typical of the everyday world outside the classroom, whereas many of the linguistic demands of the classroom reflect communication which is closer to the context-reduced end of the continuum" (p. 34). With hearing-impaired students, as with both hearing and hearing-impaired students from NES homes, an adequate level of interpersonal or context-embedded language and speech often misleads educators into thinking that the child is ready to learn in school; in fact the child may not have mastered the ideational function of language and thus cannot handle the context-reduced language environment of the school.

When working with hearing-impaired children from NES homes, it is important not only to assess whether the child has the surface fluency in the linguistic system of the school but also whether the child has the range of functions—in both the home and school languages—that will allow him or her to function successfully in school. In terms of developing a program for hearing-impaired children from NES homes, Halliday's (1974) suggestion (intended for hearing students from English-speaking homes) provides a useful guideline: "A minimum requirement for an educationally relevant approach to language is that it takes account of the child's own linguistic experience, defining this experience in terms of its richest potential and noting where there may be differences of orientation which could cause certain children difficulties in school" (p. 19).

The linguistic issues surrounding the education of linguistically and culturally diverse hearing-impaired students are not simple, and solutions to their educational and communicative problems likewise will not be simple. One must take into account these students' prior linguistic experience and abilities, recognize the role of these experiences in their cognitive and second language growth, and recognize the complexity of language functioning in school. Then one can one begin to assess and educate these students appropriately.

Language Assessment

The first task for the educator or clinician in preparing for language and educational intervention with the hearing-impaired child from an NES home is the task of language assessment. To evaluate the child's language ability appropriately, one must first ask the general question, What is the nature of the thing to be tested? (For a general discussion of bilingual assessment, see Erickson & Omark, 1981.) In potential bilingual situations, the key areas of assessment are language dominance and language proficiency. Hernandez-Chavez, Burt, and Dulay (1978), in an article on language dominance and proficiency testing, note that three parameters of language proficiency need to be examined: linguistic components, modality, and socio-linguistic performance. Because the child has a hearing impairment and usually an associated language delay, the level of the language the child has reached must also be assessed. It is important to differentiate between developmental level and proficiency, with the former being a description of the language itself and the latter an assessment of how those language abilities are used.

Given the need to assess developmental level, language dominance, and proficiency in whatever language systems exist, the choices of where and how to start and what instruments to use become far less difficult than they may appear initially. Because one is looking at a broad range of language abilities, there is no need for the use of so-called psycholinguistic assessment instruments. Use of these instruments with hearing-impaired children in general is a questionable practice because the correlation between the specific abilities tested and those abilities that underlie language acquisition has not been established (cf. Bloom & Lahey, 1978). Using these instruments with a child from another culture is even more questionable because the form of the task itself may well be outside the child's experience. This is especially true of recent immigrant children whose unfamiliarity with the task produces such low performance levels that the children are often mislabeled. In addition, these instruments are said to be nonverbal but in practice are not. They do utilize language. The fact that the child's prior language experience may be in direct contrast to the language of the test is often ignored.

In focusing on language itself, rather than on so-called processing tasks, it is also important to specify which aspects of the child's linguistic performance are most indicative of the developmental level of the child's language and are most useful in determining dominance or proficiency. Vocabulary testing, even in translation, is not an adequate linguistic measure, nor should it be used to indicate mental age in assessing hearing-impaired children from other cultures and language backgrounds. Vocabulary reflects the cultural and educational level of a speaker, not his or her linguistic level. In terms of the linguistic components that are meaningful in language assessment, Hernandez-Chavez et al. (1978) note that "grammar—the morphology and syntax—[is] best understood in terms of developmental processes and, at least for the present, provides the most adequate research and methodological basis for making judgment about levels of language proficiency" (p. 51). A growing body of knowledge in semantics and pragmatics also allows us to add those two areas to the list of linguistic components that are important to assess.

Depending on the child's background—recency of arrival, language status of the home (monolingual or bilingual), previous educational experience—the choice is made whether first to assess developmental level or dominance. If the child is a recent immigrant and from a totally NES home, then the question of dominance is answered, for surely there is no acquisition of English without exposure to it. If the child is from a bilingual background or has had some schooling in English, then dominance might be addressed first.

Dominance essentially is the question of which language is the child's stronger language. Dominance testing must also take into account how the child's abilities compare across language domains. It is not uncommon, for example, to find that hearing-impaired students with severe losses are dominant in different domains. Because most of their education has been in English, their dominant language for learning is English. However, when one considers the fluency and intelligibility of their speech—especially in the area of suprasegmental phonology—they are clearly not dominant in English for interpersonal use. Older hearing-impaired children are often more proficient in context-embedded (interpersonal) communication in the home language but, because of prior educational experience, more proficient in context-reduced (ideational) language in English. On the other hand, many young (3- to 5-year-old) children with moderate hearing impairments who come from bilingual backgrounds often indicate a level of context-embedded social communication in English that misleads educators and evaluators—they think the children are ready to function in school in English when that is really not the case. These relative abilities should be seen not as conflicts but rather as strengths that can be utilized in the student's educational development.

Assessment of the child's developmental level in language should be a descriptive one in the case of all hearing-impaired children, and a hearing-impaired child from a NES home presents only a variation of the same process that would be used to do a descriptive language evaluation of any other hearing-impaired child. Blackwell, Engen, Fischgrund, and Zarcadoolas (1978) argue convincingly that use of normative data in language assessments of hearing-impaired students is of minimal interest and utility in developing and placing students in an appropriate language education program. They also present a framework for describing the language of hearing-impaired children. This approach focuses on what the children have developed as opposed to attempting to find deficits in the child's language. The latter approach often leads to programming through a deficit model, which seeks to address aspects of the child's language performance that are said to be deviant rather than providing an overall context for language structures and functions that have not yet been acquired or developed.

In general, assessment of the limited-English-proficient hearing-impaired child should include an elicited and spontaneous sample of the child's productive language in both home language and English, with all materials used for elicitation being similar but culturally appropriate. A comparable measure of comprehension should be used in both languages so that receptive abilities can be assessed in the individual languages and then compared to ascertain dominance and relative proficiency (cf. Engen & Engen, 1983). Assessing what linguistic abilities the child does have, as opposed to what English the child does not know, is the first step in appropriate assessment of hearing-impaired students from linguistically and culturally diverse backgrounds.

Cultural Considerations

The NES child, no matter how profound the hearing impairment, brings his or her home culture to school; it is not something that is turned off or on by leaving one door and entering another.

A major aspect, and often the first encountered, is the family's view of the handicapping condition of the child and the demands that the presence and education of the child places upon the family members. For many Hispanic families, for example, the handicap of the child can be dealt with in the context of their own community, religious orientation, and belief system. What these families cannot handle are the ways in which the school expects them to participate in the child's educational program. For the typical caretaker of the Puerto Rican hearing-impaired child, the school or clinic can be an imposing, unapproachable institution, despite the best intentions of the professionals (Lerman & Cortez, 1977). An active, culturally appropriate parent involvement program is a necessary component of any bilingual/bicultural program for hearing-impaired children if parental understanding, cooperation, and support are to be expected. The culturally diverse parent is not a parent who does not care; most often this parent is simply one who does not understand what is being asked of him or her.

A major task for hearing-impaired children is that of coming to terms with the culture of their home and that of their school and peers. Rather than assuming that the child is confused and thus should be presented with only one cultural (and linguistic) model, Blackwell and Fischgrund (see Chapter 11) argue that the problem facing the hearing-impaired child is that he or she does not have enough conceptual data to understand the differences between the home and school cultures and his or her own place as a developing bicultural person. School curricula generally focus on information that is said to be central to the mainstream of North American culture, but for the child who does not have an early grasp of what that mainstream is, there is no conceptual framework with which to assimilate new information. As a result, the child is often placed in a position of knowing only that something is different. With some unintentional but powerful peer influence, the child often concludes that what is different—namely his or her parents and home life—is inferior. For such a hearing-impaired child to come to terms with a bicultural environment there needs to be a meaningful organization of information. This is the goal of a bicultural curriculum.

Overlapping the purely cultural conditions are the socioeconomic difficulties in which many NES families find themselves. The families' priorities are a function of their social and economic status. If they are poor, newly arrived immigrants, one can be sure that regular visits to the otologist, hearing aids, or individualized education plan (IEP) meetings are not high on the priority list, especially in the light of necessities like food, clothing, and adequate shelter. Special education program staff, in their desire to begin intervention relative to the child's handicap, often assume that the families' socioeconomic condition is satisfactory or, if problematical, not the school's business. Lerman and Fischgrund (1980) argue that "working with children from poor, immigrant families requires a new role for the school" and that the view that "limits the school's responsibilities to the activities of the children to the school day...leads to large numbers of dropouts and unserved children" (p. 10).

Challenges in Education

Cultural pluralism still appears to be a fact of U.S. life. Despite an overall impression that the waves of immigration of the early twentieth century are over, much cultural and linguistic diversity is still present in the U.S. today. This is of course reflected in educational institutions and no less in educational programs for the hearing impaired.

Language also appears to be the critical factor in educating all children from culturally and linguistically diverse homes and is no less critical in programs for the hearing impaired. For these children to have equal access to educational opportunity, programs addressing the issues outlined in the preceding pages need to be developed. One such program is Projecto Oportunidad, the bilingual/bicultural program at the Rhode Island School for the Deaf. Other programs for the hearing impaired are currently being developed. With careful attention to the complex linguistic and sensitive cultural issues involved, there is hope that these programs can change the depressed achievement levels of hearing-impaired students from NES homes (Jensema, 1975; Lerman & Cortez, 1977; Delgado, 1981).

A guiding proposition in bilingual/bicultural education is that the child's home language and culture can be a positive or negative factor in the child's education but never a neutral factor. Certainly no educator wishes to promote a negative factor, and attempts to neutralize by ignoring the child's home language and culture are doomed to fail. The challenge for educators of hearing-impaired children from culturally and linguistically diverse homes is to utilize that cultural and linguistic richness in the most positive fashion, for the benefit not only of those particular students and their families but of all hearing-impaired students.

References

Blackwell, P., Engen, E., Fischgrund, J., & Zarcadoolas, C. *Sentences and other systems: A language and learning curriculum for hearing-impaired students.* Washington, D.C.: A.G. Bell Association for the Deaf, 1978.

Bloom, L., & Lahey, M. *Language development and language disorders.* New York: Wiley, 1978.

Bolen, D. Issues relating to language choice: Hearing-impaired infants from bilingual homes. *VoltaReview,* 1981, *83,* 410–412.

Cummins, J. Linguistic interdependence and the educational development of bilingual children. *Review of Educational Research,* 1979, *49,* 222–251.

Cummins, J. Four misconceptions about language proficiency in bilingual education. *NABE Journal,* 1981, *5*(3), 31–45.

Delgado, G. Hearing-impaired children from non-native language homes. *American Annals of the Deaf,* 1981, *126,* 118–121. An adaptation of this article may be found on pages 28–36.

Engen, E., & Engen, T. *Rhode Island test of language comprehension.* Baltimore: University Park Press, 1983.

Erickson, J., & Omark, D. *Communication assessment of the bilingual bicultural child.* Baltimore: University Park Press, 1981.

Halliday, M.A.K. *Explorations in the functions of language.* London: Edward Arnold, 1974.

Hernandez-Chavez, E., Burt, M., & Dulay, H. Language dominance and proficiency testing: Some general considerations. *NABE Journal,* 1978, 3(1), 41–54.

Hurd, A. Letter to Harold S. Bucklin, May 3, 1921. Rhode Island School for the Deaf Archives.

Jensema, C. *The relationship between academic achievement and the demographic characteristics of hearing-impaired youth.* Washington, D.C.: Gallaudet College Office of Demographic Studies, 1975.

Lerman, A., & Cortez, E. *Discovering and meeting the needs of Hispanic hearing-impaired children* (Report, CREED VII project). New York: Lexington School for the Deaf, 1977.

Lerman, A., & Fischgrund, J. Improving services to Hispanic hearing-impaired students and their families. Paper presented at the 9th Annual Meeting of NABE, Anaheim, April 1980.

9

Language and/or System Assessment for Spanish/Deaf Preschoolers

Barbara Luetke-Stahlman and Frederick F. Weiner

The effective education of Hispanic deaf students has become a more apparent need in recent years due to the increasing number of Hispanic people in the United States. Enrollment of Hispanic hearing-impaired students in residential schools for the deaf increased 25.4 percent from 1972 to 1977 (Maestas, 1981). During the 1978–79 school year, Hispanics accounted for 9.4 percent of the total hearing-impaired population (Moores, 1981).

To meet the growing needs of Hispanic deaf students, a few innovative programs have evolved in this country. These programs have been based primarily on models of education taken from the field of bilingual education.

Basically, the proponents of bilingual education advocate that bilingual children should be educated in their first language and then, after a gradual transition, in English. While this approach seems straightforward when teaching normal-hearing children, the task is much more complicated when it is applied to hearing-impaired children. Specifically, the major problem becomes the determination of a first language on which to build English literacy skills. Depending upon the degree of hearing loss and the assimilation of the family into the English-speaking society, Spanish may not function as the first language for hearing-impaired children of normal-hearing Hispanic parents. In such cases, the language used as a first language in the bilingual education model could be combinations of Spanish, English, and any one of various sign languages and/or systems. Therefore, it seems apparent that one's heritage, whether that heritage be Hispanic or deaf, does not automatically fix the first language or the language to be used in bilingual education models.

The purpose of our investigation was not to examine the bilingual transition model of education. This model has been examined elsewhere (e.g., Troike, 1978). Rather, our purpose was to determine a "first language" that should be selected to teach language concepts to Hispanic hearing-impaired children whose parents are Spanish-speaking and/or members of the Hispanic community in the United States. We were interested in determining whether these children were homogeneous with respect to this first language and could therefore be grouped together in the classroom setting. Specifically our question was: Given the languages and/or systems (L/S) of English, English-sign mix, Spanish, Spanish-sign mix, and sign alone, do any of these five L/S more efficiently facilitate the acquisition of receptive knowledge of noun, verb, and adjective vocabularies?

Subjects

Three Hispanic deaf females enrolled in the St. Christopher's Hospital Nursery program for hearing-impaired preschoolers in Philadelphia were subjects for this investigation. The program consisted of a parent-infant class and two classrooms primarily for three- and four-year-olds, respectively. Children attended school approximately five hours a day and engaged in structured activities aimed primarily at language development.

Subject 1 had been attending the program since her fourth birthday approximately four months earlier. She had a bilateral, profound, (unaided) sensorineural hearing loss. Her teacher judged her to benefit minimally from the use of her hearing aid, yet she wore it consistently. (See Appendix for a copy of the Teacher Rating Survey.) The child communicated primarily through a sign and voice mix but also used gesture. Her family had emigrated from Puerto Rico. She lived with her parents and a five-year-old sister, all of whom had normal hearing. Her mother used sign and oral English to communicate with her. The family did not want the daughter to use Spanish in school.

Subject 2 was three years, five months old. The child and mother attended the parent-infant program during the 1979–80 academic year, and the child had been enrolled in the three-year-old classroom approximately six months. She had a bilateral, moderate-to-severe, (unaided) sensorineural hearing loss. The child had a hearing aid but refused to wear it. The teacher reported that the child had good unaided hearing. She communicated primarily through a sign and voice mix, but also used gesture and voice alone. Her family had emigrated from Puerto Rico. She lived with her hearing parents and six siblings, two of whom were also hearing impaired. Her mother used sign, gesture, oral Spanish, and oral English to communicate with her. The teacher reported that Subject 2's parents spoke primarily Spanish, while her older, hearing siblings spoke primarily English.

Subject 3 was four years, eleven months old and had been enrolled in school for approximately six months. She had a moderate-to-severe, (unaided) sensorineural hearing loss. This child consistently wore a hearing aid and was judged by her teacher as having good aided hearing. Her unaided hearing was judged as poor. She communicated primarily through sign and voice mixed with fingerspelling. She used both oral English and/or Spanish, but use of speech decreased when she communicated with peers. Subject 3's family came from Puerto Rico. The family's communication was primarily in English alone, but Spanish alone, sign, and English-sign mix were also used.

Languages and/or Systems

The languages and/or systems (L/S) selected for study were those that are potentially available in school programs educating hearing-impaired children from Spanish-speaking homes. The investigation inputs were oral English alone, English-sign mix, oral Spanish alone, Spanish-sign mix, and sign alone.

The first author produced the oral English, oral Spanish, and signs used in the study. The English reflected a midwestern dialect. The Spanish was that of a non-native speaker. The signs were a combination of American Sign Language (ASL) and signed English. (No Spanish sign language was used in the study.) All signs were reviewed by two trained interpreters at the St. Christopher's Hospital Nursery program so that all stimulus questions were presented in the hospital's sign dialect. The sign-alone phrases were presented without voice.

Noun Vocabulary Task

Stimuli. The stimuli consisted of 30 Rebus Glossary Cards (Clark, 1974). Twenty were selected as training stimuli and 10 as probe items. The 20 training stimuli were randomly divided into 5 L/S groups of 4 rebus cards each. Each learning trial was defined as a random presentation of the 4 nouns in each L/S, presented 3 times each, for a total of 12 per L/S. The 10 probe items were also randomly divided into 5 L/S groups of 2 rebuses each. Probe items served as controls and therefore were not taught. The probe condition was administered during baseline, after every third trial, and after criterion was achieved for any L/S.

Baseline. Because of the age and attention span of the subjects, it was decided that an abbreviated baseline condition would be administered. The purpose of the baseline was to ensure that each subject did not know any of the vocabulary items via any L/S. In the event that a vocabulary item was known, that item was eliminated from the training items. Because a routine baseline designed to meet the objectives above would have required at least 60 items presented via 5 L/S for a total of 300 responses—plus the probe condition items presented via the 5 L/S for a total of 50 presentations—a compromise was sought. The compromise was to use only one baseline trial, keep the baseline sessions short, and test all vocabulary in three L/S (English alone, Spanish alone, and sign alone). It was felt that the use of only one baseline trial was justified because the initial training trial could also be evaluated as a quasi-baseline due to the minimal amount of training that would have occurred at the time. The compromise of using three L/S in the baseline condition was decided after pilot testing demonstrated that the subjects would have a great deal of difficulty attending to 350 nonreinforced responses. The English-sign mix and Spanish-sign mix conditions were eliminated because they were combinations of the two primary languages and the sign-alone condition. Baseline stimuli were presented with no teaching or reinforcement for correct responses.

All subjects were taught individually in a familiar room at the school. The order in which the investigator worked with each subject and the order in which each L/S was taught were counterbalanced to control for time-of-day effects.

The basic strategy was to allow subjects an opportunity to demonstrate which L/S was the most efficient for increasing receptive vocabulary ability. The teaching strategy was employed in a game-like situation in which the investigator placed a stimulus and three distractor items in front of the subject and asked a stimulus question in the appropriate L/S. Responses were accepted if the subject pointed to or placed a small toy on the correct item. Correct was defined as a correct identification within five seconds after the investigator made the request. Incorrect was defined as an incorrect identification or failure to respond within five seconds.

Table 1
Question Stimuli and Their Distractors for Subject 1 on Task 1.

Language/System	Question Stimuli	Distractors
English	Where is the carrot? Where is the camera? Where is the balloon? Where is the camel?	The stimuli and distractors are presented via rebuses (Clark, 1974). The other three cards in the set acted as distractors for the stimuli being tested.
English-sign mix	Where is the ghost? 　　S　　　S Where is the rooster? 　　S　　　S Where is the dentist? 　　S　　　S Where is the napkin? 　　S　　　S	
Spanish	¿Dónde está la cadena? ¿Dónde está la abeja? ¿Dónde está el espanto? ¿Dónde está el nube?	(chain) (bee) (scarecrow) (cloud)
Spanish-sign mix	¿Dónde está el melon? 　　S　　　S ¿Dónde está la canasta? 　　S　　　S ¿Dónde está el oso? 　　S　　　S ¿Dónde está el periodico? 　　S　　　S	(melon) (basket) (bear) (newspaper)
Sign alone	WHERE PLATE WHERE WHERE PEAR WHERE WHERE LAKE WHERE WHERE HELICOPTER WHERE	

Note. A signed word is denoted either by the letter *S* or by capitalization throughout.

If a subject made an incorrect response during the training sessions, the investigator assisted in the learning of the task by modeling the correct response and allowing the subject to imitate it and/or physically guiding the subject's hand to touch the correct item. An initially correct response or a correct response after investigator intervention (scored as incorrect) was rewarded with stickers, nail polish, peanuts, clapping, etc. Actual stimulus questions appear in Luetke-Stahlman (1982). Examples of question stimuli and their distractors for Subject 1 are presented in Table 1. Vocabulary training continued until a subject correctly responded to 9 of 12 items for two consecutive trials in any one L/S.

Verb Vocabulary Task

Stimuli. The stimuli in this task consisted of 30 four-inch-square color pictures of action words taken from Betts Basic Readers (1965). Twenty pictures were again randomly divided into five L/S groups of four pictures each. Each learning trial was defined as a random presentation of the 4 action words in each L/S, 3 times each, for a total of 12 items per condition. The remaining 10 items were used as the probe. These items were randomly divided into five L/S groups of two items each. Probe items served as controls and therefore were not taught. The probe was administered during baseline, after every third trial, and after criterion was achieved for one L/S.

Baseline and Training. The basic baseline and training procedure described for the noun vocabulary task was again employed. The purpose was to ensure that each subject did not know any of the vocabulary items via any L/S. Stimulus questions appear in Luetke-Stahlman (1982).

Adjective Vocabulary Task

Stimuli. The stimuli were 30 pictures of nouns obtained from Betts Basic Readers (1965). Twenty pictures were randomly divided into five L/S groups of four cards each. Each learning trial was again defined as a random presentation of the 4 nouns in each L/S, 3 times each, for a total of 12 items per L/S. The 10 probe items were also randomly divided into 5 L/S groups of 2 pictures each. A trial was defined as a random presentation of each of the 10 stimuli (2 items per L/S).

Baseline and Training. The basic baseline and training procedures described in the noun vocabulary task were again employed. The teaching strategy was to allow subjects an opportunity to demonstrate which training condition was the most efficient for increasing receptive adjective vocabulary ability for each subject. The stimulus questions appear in Luetke-Stahlman (1982).

Experimental Design

To determine the relative efficiencies of the five L/S in facilitating various language behaviors, a modification of a multiple baseline design (Birnbauer, Peterson, & Solnick, 1974) was utilized. In this design, five input languages and/or systems (the five L/S) were utilized to teach various vocabulary skills. Other vocabulary items from each of the five L/S were withheld from treatment to serve as a probe control. Verification of the positive effects of treatment in this design was possible if vocabulary ability improved in any of the L/S while there was no improvement in the corresponding nontreatment probe condition. If this were the case then the improvement in vocabulary of each L/S was in fact due to training, and the relative differences between vocabulary acquisition in each L/S could then be compared.

Results

Acquisition curves were constructed for each subject's performance on each of the three vocabulary types studied. The standard analysis technique in single subject research of visual inspection (Baer, Wolf, & Risley, 1968) was utilized. The assumption behind visual inspection is that unless differences in results were obviously apparent, these results are not educationally significant. Statistical procedures have sometimes been used, but in doing so many of the assumptions behind the procedures are violated (Kazdin, 1976).

Subject 1

Noun Vocabulary. Acquisition curves for Subject 1 showed a consistent pattern of performance for noun vocabulary learning. She performed best on vocabulary items taught using English-sign mix (ESM), Spanish-sign mix (SSM), and sign alone (SA). Poorest performance was on vocabulary items taught using oral English (OE) and oral Spanish (OS). At the same time, there was no corresponding improvement in the probe condition, showing that improvement in ESM, SSM, and SA was due to training. Therefore, it seemed as though signed instruction was essential for Subject 1 to learn noun vocabulary.

Verb Vocabulary. Acquisition curves for verb vocabulary learning for Subject 1 also showed preferences for ESM, SSM, and SA—the ones involving the sign modality. Vocabulary learning for OE and OS was negligible. Furthermore, there was no improvement in the probe condition, showing that improvement in verb vocabulary, as in noun vocabulary, was due to the use of sign.

Adjective Vocabulary. Acquisition curves for adjective vocabulary learning for Subject 1 showed negligible adjective vocabulary learning in the oral-only L/A of OE and OS. Vocabulary acquisition occurred only if sign was a component in the L/S. The probe condition showed no corresponding improvement, certifying that sign was a significant factor in adjective vocabulary learning.

Subject 2

Noun Vocabulary. Acquisition curves for Subject 2's noun vocabulary learning appear in Figure 1. She showed improvement in noun vocabulary for all L/S except oral English. There was no corresponding improvement in the probe condition, showing that improvement in the other L/S was due to training. These results showed that either sign and/or Spanish was necessary for vocabulary improvement.

Verb Vocabulary. Like the previous results, there was some improvement in vocabulary ability if Spanish or sign was a component in the L/S used in training. Greatest improvement occurred when both Spanish and sign were used in combination (SSM). At the same time, there was no improvement in the probe condition, which was essential to show that improvement in each L/S was due to training.

Figure 1
Rate of noun vocabulary acquisition for Subject 2 in each of five languages and/or systems

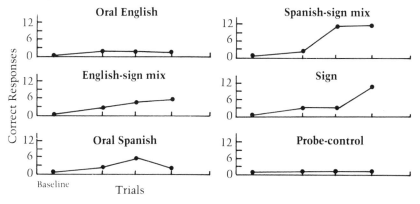

Figure 2
Rate of verb vocabulary acquisition for Subject 3 in each of five languages and/or systems

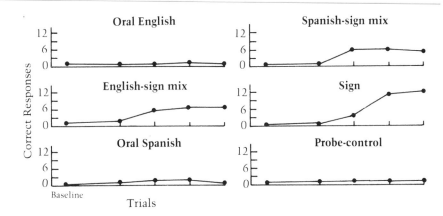

Adjective Vocabulary. Because of the length of time needed to reach criterion for noun and verb vocabulary, this task was not presented to Subject 2.

Subject 3

Noun Vocabulary. Results for Subject 3 were somewhat mixed on noun vocabulary. There was some noun vocabulary learning for all L/S except oral English. The greatest amount of learning appeared to occur with SSM and SA. There was no corresponding improvement in the probe condition.

Verb Vocabulary. Results of verb vocabulary acquisition (see Figure 2) were somewhat different from noun vocabulary acquisition for Subject 3. Here the two oral L/S (OE, OS) showed negligible improvement. The three L/S involving sign (ESM, SSM, SA) showed the greatest improvement. Again, there was no corresponding improvement in the probe conditions.

Adjective Vocabulary. Acquisition curves for adjective vocabulary showed that learning occurred with all L/S except oral Spanish. The sign-alone L/S showed the most adjective vocabulary learning. The probe condition resulted in no improvement, showing that improvement in other L/S was due to the specific L/S utilized.

Discussion

The data indicate that the three subjects demonstrated three different L/S preferences for learning noun, verb, and adjective vocabulary items. Subject 1 could be characterized as demonstrating sign as the most efficient L/S. She performed poorly on the vocabulary tasks taught through oral English and oral Spanish. Her best performance came when sign alone was used or when it was combined with English or Spanish. This finding was consistent with the fact that this child had a profound, bilateral, sensorineural hearing loss and was reported to benefit minimally from the use of a hearing aid. For Subject 1, then, neither her Spanish heritage nor any exposure to a second language (i.e., English) facilitated vocabulary learning. Instead, her deafness was the significant factor.

Subject 2 completed the noun and verb vocabulary tasks but did not have time to participate in the adjective vocabulary task. On the basis of results obtained for noun vocabulary, it would appear that Subject 2 could learn through oral Spanish or sign. Most likely, vocabulary acquisition using an English-sign mix was due to the sign component, because performance was so poor for the English-alone condition. These results were predictable from the case history. Subject 2's moderate-to-severe hearing loss enabled her to learn through an oral-only language (Spanish). Her inability to learn through English alone was predicted from the fact that her parents spoke primarily Spanish at home. For Subject 2, heritage and handicap seemed significant in determining which L/S facilitated vocabulary learning.

Subject 3's behavior on the assessment tasks presented the most mixed results. For the noun and verb vocabulary tasks, she seemed to present a similar learning pattern to Subject 1, for whom sign or sign-mix produced the greatest learning. In the adjective vocabulary task, however, oral English-alone seemed to produce as much learning as sign or sign-mix. This inconsistent pattern, however, could be predicted from the case history. That is, her hearing loss was only moderate-to-severe and improved significantly when she wore her hearing aid. Furthermore, the mother was English-dominant while the father and caretaker spoke Spanish. Given her improved, aided hearing, she was exposed to a great deal of English at both home and school. For Subject 3, then, heritage played no role in predicting which L/S would facilitate learning. Instead, her deafness and her exposure to an English-speaking society were educationally significant.

Educational Implications

This study illustrated that neither heritage nor etiological classification dictate a specific language used by Hispanic deaf students. Depending on the amount of residual hearing they are able to utilize and the amount of Spanish spoken in their families, some Hispanic deaf children may speak and comprehend Spanish while others may not. Minority deaf children should be afforded the opportunity to demonstrate which of the potential languages and/or systems are beneficial to them in learning academic-related skills. The instructional language and/or system used as the primary method of instruction should then be determined by evaluating four variables:

1. The language and/or system of the primary caretaker(s)

2. The amount of exposure to sign languages and/or systems at home or in school

3. The child's degree of hearing loss and level of usable, aided hearing

4. The language and/or system that the child demonstrates to be the most effective for learning

While English literacy skills are obviously the goal of education in the United States, English immersion is not the only model by which to achieve that goal with hearing-impaired children from Spanish-speaking families. Some Hispanic deaf children may achieve reading and writing skills more efficiently when teachers utilize oral Spanish and/or Spanish paired with sign as instructional input modes. This possibility was demonstrated by Subjects 2 and 3 in this study.

Finally, the variable of cultural identity may not be significant in educating some Hispanic deaf students. Results from training Subject 1 illustrated that sign-alone may be the most beneficial instructional input mode when teaching prelingually, profoundly deaf students.

Conclusion

To program effectively for the increasing number of hearing-impaired children from Spanish-speaking homes in the United States, educators in the field of hearing impairment need to determine how language proficiency assessment and classroom placement regarding hearing, bilingual students can be applied and adapted to fit the needs of Hispanic deaf students. When a hearing, bilingual student from an oral, bilingual home in the United States enters school today, placement is usually in a classroom using English-only or bilingual instruction, based primarily on the child's proficiency in oral English. English-dominant children are placed in English-only classrooms and bilingual or Spanish-dominant children are placed in transitional programs. If a child is hearing impaired, however, placement is usually in an oral or simultaneous communication classroom, assuming there is parental consent.

Based on empirical evidence from research conducted with hearing, minority-language students, Cummins (1979, 1980) argued that such students obtained English literacy skills more proficiently if their home language was used as the vehicle of instruction. Cummins also found that majority-language students learned a second language most effectively via the minority language; i.e., no student's first language suffered if instruction was offered only via the minority language. Cummins concluded that the transition of these students into English-only classrooms made no logical sense. (See Luetke-Stahlman, 1982, for a more comprehensive investigation of the Cummins model as applied to literacy skills in hearing-impaired students.)

The Cummins model suggested that hearing-impaired students should also be instructed in their minority language. However, the minority language of a hearing-impaired child from a Spanish-speaking home may not be identical to that of his or her parents; the minority language may vary among such children. Although the child may in fact acquire the rudiments of Spanish as a first language, the child may also use sign in conjunction with, or independent of, the Spanish. Given this assumption, Hispanic deaf children must be afforded the opportunity to demonstrate which of all L/S is a first language. The identified L/S should then be the one utilized to teach English literacy skills to that child in the classroom (Cummins, 1980). Other L/S that are used in instruction and found to benefit other students will not cause the first language acquisition of any child in the class to suffer; this is true even when students with different first languages are mixed in a classroom and different languages and/or systems for instruction are utilized with specific students (Cummins, 1980).

Further research is necessary to determine the extent to which the Cummins model is adaptable to programs for hearing-impaired Hispanic students and whether such adaptation is financially feasible. In any case, this study highlights the fact that strong differences in language skills exist among students who share hearing impairment and minority cultural background. Such individual differences deserve much more attention in educational research and practice.

References

Baer, D. M., Wolf, M. M., & Risley, T. R. Some current dimensions of applied behavior analysis. *Journal of Applied Behavior Analysis,* 1968, *1*, 91–97.

Betts Basic Readers. New York: American Book, 1965.

Birnbauer, K., Peterson, C., & Solnick, J. Design and interpretation of studies of single subjects. *American Journal of Mental Deficiency*, 1974, *29*, 191–203.

Clark, C. *Rebus glossary cards.* Circle Pines, Minn.: American Guidance, 1974.

Cummins, J. Cognitive/academic language proficiency, linguistic interdependence, the optimum age question and some other matters. *Working Papers in Bilingualism,* 1979, *19*, 197–205.

Cummins, J. The entry and exit fallacy in bilingual education. *NABE Journal,* 1980, *4*, 25–60.

Kazdin, A. E. Statistical analysis for single case experimental designs. In M. Hersen & D. Barlow (Eds.), *Single-case experimental designs.* New York: Pergamon Press, 1976.

Luetke-Stahlman, B. *Training receptive language response abilities to assess language and/or system preferences of preschool hearing-impaired children from Spanish-speaking homes.* Unpublished doctoral dissertation, Pennsylvania State University, 1982.

Maestas, J. *Hispanic professionals in special education.* Paper presented at Virginia Union University, June 1981.

Moores, D. F. Personal communication, May 1981.

Troike, R. Research evidence for the effectiveness of bilingual education. *NABE Journal,* 1978, *3*, 13–24.

Appendix

Teacher Rating Survey

1. Subject's name _____

2. Exact age_____, as of_____(date)

   Please circle the correct response below and provide *any* additional information that you feel is appropriate.

3. The subject wears a hearing aid at school.

   yes   sometimes   always

4. The subject's use of his/her *unaided* hearing is

   good   poor   undeterminable

5. The subject's use of his/her *aided* hearing is

   good   poor   undeterminable

6. The subject has been in your class _____ months.

7. The subject has been in any school program _____ months.

8. Socio-economically, the subject appears to be

   very poor   poor   low middle class   high middle class

   (parents unemployed)   (blue collar workers)   (professionals)

9. How would you rate the quality of this subject's academic work *when compared to other students in your class?*

   below class level   at class level   above class level

10. Does the subject appear to have any learning problems in addition to his/her hearing impairment? (LD, vision, glasses, etc.)

    yes;_____(which ones)   no

11. How do you usually communicate with the subject?

    Circle all that apply, but star the major manner.

    voice alone   writing   sign alone   gesture   sign and voice mixed

    fingerspelling   ASL   other:_____

12. How do you usually communicate with the subject's parents?

    no communication

    English by phone____, note____, meetings ____, home visit____

    Spanish via an interpreter

13. Are there any Spanish-speaking staff in your program?

    yes   no

14. Do you think Spanish-speaking staff are needed in your program?

    yes   no

15. As far as *you know*, which languages and/or modes are used in the home *with the subject?* (Circle all that apply, but star the major manner.)

    Spanish alone   English alone   writing   fingerspelling

    ASL   gesture   Sign-Spanish mix   Sign-English mix

    other:_____

16. Does the subject have any Spanish friends at school?

    yes   no

17. Which colors does the subject know: _____

    _____

    How does he/she *respond to or express* them? _____

    _____

18. Which numbers does the subject know: _____

_____

How does he/she respond to or express them? _____

_____

19. Which nouns does the subject know: _____

_____

How does he/she respond to or express them? _____

_____

20. Which shapes does the subject know: _____

_____

How does he/she respond to or express them? _____

_____

21. Which verbs does the subject know:_____

_____

How does he/she respond to or express them? _____

_____

22. Does the subject usually sign one, two, or three word phrases?

_____

23. Did the subject use any Spanish upon entry into your classroom?

yes   no

24. Do you think the subject *could* use Spanish at school?

yes   no

25. Do you think the subject *should* use Spanish at school (as a base language for learning manual or oral English)?

yes   no

Assessment

10

Assessment of Hispanic Children: Implications for Hispanic Hearing-Impaired Children

Richard A. Figueroa, Gilbert L. Delgado, and Nadeen T. Ruiz

The National Center for Education Statistics estimates that there are 3.5 million linguistic-minority school-age children who are "limited English proficient" (LEP). Most of these come from Spanish-speaking homes. Assuming that these estimates are accurate and that the prevalence of hearing impairments is comparable to that of the U.S. population, i.e., 0.575 percent (Blackhurst & Berdine, 1981), the total number of LEP, Hispanic hearing impaired may well approximate 20,000. However, this may be an underestimation since there is substantial controversy about the size of the Hispanic population in the U.S. (Waggoner, 1978). Delgado (see chapter 3) has shown that most schools and programs for the hearing impaired report an increase in children from non-native-language homes. This study also revealed that of the total population of hearing-impaired children surveyed, 30 percent were identified as multihandicapped, whereas of the *non-native* language groups, 50 percent were considered multihandicapped. These data present a clear and direct challenge to special educators in the United States. This article focuses on one dimension of the challenge: How are these children to be assessed?

Background

Except for the work of Zieziula (1982), there is no substantive literature on testing Hispanic hearing-impaired (HHI) or limited English-proficient, Hispanic hearing-impaired (LEP/HHI) children. The same applies to testing Hispanic LEP children. There is, however, extensive literature on testing Hispanic children (DeBlassie, 1980; Padilla & Ruiz,

1973; Samuda, 1975). Until recently, most of this literature concentrated almost exclusively on the problems associated with such testing. Lately studies have appeared purporting to show that, on various psychometric criteria, tests are not biased with Hispanic pupils (Dean, 1977a, 1977b, 1979; Reynolds, 1982). Sattler (1982), in fact, repeatedly suggests that tests are all right *as they are*. Because similar assertions can be made about tests presently in use with Anglo-American hearing-impaired children—i.e., that it is valid to use them on HHI or LEP/HHI—a brief overview of the background of testing Hispanic children is in order. If for no other reason, one would hope that a quick historical review might help those faced with the assessment of HHI and LEP/HHI children to avoid the mistakes of the past.

The net effect of the psychological community's unwillingness to heed Hispanic psychologists warnings (Sanchez, 1932a, 1932b, 1934) was dramatically documented by Mercer. In one location in California, 32 percent of the educable mentally retarded (EMR) school population were Hispanic children, although they constituted only 9.5 percent of the total school population. Most of the children were labeled as EMR mainly on the basis of IQ scores, and in great part because of a significantly depressed verbal (English) IQ. Their out-of-school functioning was not evaluated. They were EMR only in school. When Mercer did take their out-of-school adaptivity into account (using a test of adaptive behavior), she found that the incidence of Hispanics labeled as EMR dropped by 60 percent (Mercer, 1972). The results of Mercer's (1973) landmark study were not confined to Riverside, the place where the investigation took place. Other data indicated that the problem existed in many areas of the country (U.S. Commission on Civil Rights, 1974).

In the early 1970s, the federal courts intervened. Several court cases addressed the problems reported by Mercer and others. *Diana v. California* (1970) is perhaps the most critical of the testing cases. *Lau v. Nichols* (1974) is the most important with respect to instruction.

Diana addressed issues and practices extant in the U.S. testing community since the 1930s. It laid down some landmark directives for testing LEP children, and it continues to exert influence and pressure on California regarding the entire matter of valid and appropriate diagnostic testing of Hispanic and other culturally and linguistically different children.

The plaintiffs in *Diana*, nine rural Mexican-American children and their parents, filed an elaborate set of complaints before Judge Robert

Peckham of the Ninth District Court in 1970. The complaints addressed virtually every important issue in Hispanic psychoeducational testing, including claims that:

1. The case and its issues fell within the jurisdiction of the 14th Amendment (procedural and substantive due process), the Civil Rights Act of 1964, the Elementary and Secondary Education Act, and the statutes under the Constitution and laws of California.

2. Placement in these classes caused irreparable damage in terms of illiteracy and stigma.

3. IQ tests (Binet or WISC) were typically administered between the ages of four to eight years of age, to measure certain children's intellectual ability in order to determine EMR placement (IQ range 55–70).

4. The children were not mentally retarded. They were tested in the wrong language.

5. The IQ norms used were not valid insofar as they assumed that children of the same age had the same type and the same quality of education.

6. Because of their atypical learning experiences, and their low SES status, these children's IQs had little relationship to their ability to learn.

7. Stanford-Binet IQs, because of their emphasis on English verbal skills, resulted in ridiculous scores, e.g., IQs of 30 for children who had no physiological anomalies.

8. Mexican-American children were overrepresented in the EMR classes of the county and the state, and to such a degree that it could not happen by chance.

9. The suit brought by the plaintiffs was in the nature of a class action suit on behalf of all bilingual Mexican-American children placed in EMR classes, or who will be given an IQ test.

10. The right of every child to equal education was fundamental.

11. The Civil Rights Act of 1964 ordered school districts to eliminate discrimination based on national origin and also ordered equal educational opportunity for all.

12. The argument of irreparable injury was stated on the basis of denial of equal educational opportunity and academic underachievement

resulting in poor employment status and life-long stigma for having been "mentally retarded."

Diana was settled out of court. The agreement stipulated that:

a. Children had to be tested in their own language and in English.

b. They could be tested on nonverbal sections of the tests.

c. Mexican-American children in EMR classes had to be retested and reevaluated on nonverbal test sections.

d. Districts had to submit annual summaries of the retesting efforts and their plans for transitional programs.

e. A test of IQ that reflects Mexican-American culture was to be developed and normed on Mexican-American children.

f. If there was a disparity between the racial/ethnic representation of the district and the EMR classes, to a significant degree, the districts so involved had to submit an explanation.

The *Diana* case is unique among testing cases because it provided the means by which Hispanic children's intelligence could be estimated (especially using nonverbal measures), and because it mandated the use of the child's home language in testing. Also, unlike other testing cases, there were no testing moratoriums, quotas, or concerns about nature/nurture issues in *Diana*.

In 1974, *Lau v. Nichols* was unanimously decided by the U.S. Supreme Court. The Court found it illegal to assume—simply because some 1,200 Chinese-speaking children were getting the same textbooks, teachers, curricula, and school facilities—that they were in fact receiving an equal educational opportunity. Justice Douglas wrote that "students who do not understand English are effectively foreclosed from any meaningful education." Some form of accommodation to their special language needs had to be made. Unfortunately, the Court failed to specify what this was.

For Hispanic children, *Lau* promised much since, historically, the sink-or-swim, total immersion approach has been responsible for much of the severe educational underachievement of Hispanics (U.S. Commission on Civil Rights, 1971). The actual implementation of *Lau*, however, has been mired by a highly politicized debate about bilingual education, and the relevance of *Lau* in special education testing and instruction has yet to be appreciated. Presently, children who are LEP and handicapped can be either LEP or handicapped but not both. They are eligible for either special education or bilingual education but not bilingual special education nor bilingual assessment. Though school personnel may not realize it, LEP handicapped children come under the protections of both *Lau* and Public Law 94-142.

The Status of Hispanic Assessment

In 1975, PL 94-142 tried to address the problems in testing minority children. It stated that "procedures to assure that testing and evaluation materials utilized for the purposes of evaluation and placement of handicapped children...be selected and administered so as not to be racially or culturally discriminatory." For Hispanic LEP children (as well as for hearing-impaired children) the law further ordered that "such materials or procedures shall be provided and administered in the child's native language or mode of communication unless it is *clearly* not feasible to do so..." (Sec. 612(5)(c); emphasis added). When PL 94-142 was passed there were few, if any, psychometrically sound native language tests for Hispanic children. Well-meaning school districts used nonverbal tests, or translated tests, or had their bilingual aides and secretaries do extemporaneous translations and interpretations during testing. Other districts determined that it was not feasible to do native language testing and continued to test in English, to mix verbal and nonverbal test results, and to adhere rigidly to norm-referenced outcomes.

Four years after PL 94-142, however, Mercer and Lewis (1979) published the final technical manual of the *System of Multicultural Pluralistic Assessment* (SOMPA). This, to date, is the most comprehensive battery of tests specifically aimed at doing nonbiased testing of culturally different children.

Table 1 presents the SOMPA tests. They are grouped in the three models of assessment distinguished and described by Mercer and Lewis. Each model, according to them, carries its own definitions of *normal* and *abnormal*, its own assumptions and characteristics, and its own risks. For Mercer and Lewis, many of the errors made by clinicians stem from classifying tests in the wrong model. The penchant of thinking of IQ as a biological (Medical Model) test capable of measuring genotypic potential is the most notorious example of this type of error.

The *Adaptive Behavior Inventory for Children* (ABIC) is quite likely the best measure of adaptive behavior currently available. Adaptive behavior, regrettably, is a relatively young construct. Heber (1981) first

Table 1
SOMPA Tests

Medical Model Tests	Social System Model Tests	Pluralistic Model Tests
Physical Dexterity Tasks	Adaptive Behavior Inventory for Children (ABIC)	Estimated Learning Potential (ELP)
Bender Visual Motor Gestalt Test	Family	Verbal
	Community	Performance
Weight by Height	Peer Relations	Full Scale
Visual Acuity	Nonacademic School Roles	Sociocultural Scales
Auditory Acuity	Earner/Consumer	Family Size
	Self-Maintenance	Family Structure
Health History Inventories		Socioeconomic Status
	School Functioning Level (SFL)	Urban Acculturation
	Verbal	
	Performance	
	Full Scale	

defined it as "the degree to which the individual is able to function and maintain himself independently, and...the degree to which he meets satisfactorily the culturally imposed demands of personal and social responsibility..." (p. 61). Since 1961, many tests of adaptive behavior have appeared (Coulter & Morrow, 1978). Most of them are used in conjunction with IQ to diagnose mental retardation. Adaptive behavior, it is felt, balances out this form of diagnosis by focusing attention on out-of-school competency relative to independent functioning and the acquisition of personal and social responsibility. Whether adaptive behavior tests do this is still being debated (Reschly, 1982).

The ABIC has good technical properties (Sattler, 1982). It provides an out-of-school view of the child's functioning in six social role areas (Family, Community, Peers, Nonacademic School Roles, Earner/Consumer, and Self-Maintenance). Because the test is administered to the parent, it actually measures the caretaker's perception of the child's functioning. Research on the ABIC has been sparse. The principal areas of concern, to date, have been its validation and its impact on the incidence of mild mental retardation when it is used together with IQ to define mental subnormality (Reschly, 1982). The ABIC is available in Spanish but there are no separate norms for LEP parents. There is some indication (Mercer & Lewis, 1979, p. 102; Figueroa, 1980a) that Hispanic children do not score as well as Anglo or Black children on the ABIC.

The Sociocultural Scales measure a family's distance from Anglo-American, middle class society and the family's distance from its own ethnic group. The items in the Sociocultural Scales locate a family in "sociocultural space" or the intersection of the dimensions of socioeconomic status, acculturation to Anglo-American society, and assimilation to Anglo-American society. One of the functions that the Sociocultural Scales fulfills is to adjust the IQ scores from the Wechsler Intelligence Scale for Children–Revised (WISC-R). The WISC-R appears in SOMPA's Social Sytem and Pluralistic Model Tests. In the Social System Model, the WISC-R's U.S. norms are used with all children. The test, however, is viewed more as a measure of the social "fit" of a child to the social system known as the public schools than a measure of cognitive ability. In the Pluralistic Model of assessment, the WISC-R norms are statistically adjusted so that children are compared only to children from the same ethnic group and with approximately the same sociocultural configurations (on the Sociocultural Scales). The adjusted IQ is called Estimated Learning Potential (ELP). The ELP is the most controversial part of SOMPA. It is also the most direct and bold attempt at doing "nondiscriminatory" testing.

The logic of ELP is really quite clear. For example, a Mexican child, recently arrived in the U.S., was selected to be part of the SOMPA norming study. Juan's home, culture, and language were typical of a Mexican child. Yet he had acquired enough English to take the WISC-R. On the U.S. norms he scored 111. Yet his family's Sociocultural Scale scores predicted that children from his sociocultural world would, on the average, achieve a WISC-R IQ of 81. Juan is 30 points above *his* group's average. The ELP adjusts Juan's score to reflect his standing relative to his group, i.e., 30 points above the average, or an IQ of 130.

Notwithstanding the ultimate fate of ELP's validity, the concept makes a unique contribution by underscoring the need to separate the predictive function of a test from its diagnostic function.

New Tests

Though instruments for Hispanic LEP children have been available (Pletcher et al., 1978), their use in psychodiagnostic assessment in schools has been minimal. In great part, this has been due to the lack of knowledge of diagnosticians about the existence of these instruments.

Also, some tests, like the 1951 Puerto Rican WISC, had technical properties that could not meet the testing standards proposed by the American Psychological Association. Recently, however, many new tests have become available. They cover several areas of assessment, have good-to-excellent technical properties, and have English language counterparts that are well known by school-based assessment personnel.

The Mexico City Tests. Under the direction of Dr. Margarita Gomez-Palacio, Director of Special Education in Mexico, a large norming study of most of the SOMPA tests was undertaken in 1981 in Mexico City. A random sample of 1,100 children, ages 5–11, was used to develop new norms for Spanish versions of the WISC-R, Adaptive Behavior Inventory for Children, Bender, Health History Inventories, and Sociocultural Scales. These are now published (Dirección General de Educación Especial, 1982; Gomez-Palacio, Padilla, & Roll, 1982; Gomez-Palacio, Rangel-Hinojosa, & Padilla, 1982; Subsecretaria de Educación Elemental, Dirección General de Educación Especial, 1982) albeit difficult to procure.* They uniformly have fair-to-good technical properties and provide extremely useful data on LEP children. They may not, however, be appropriate for all LEP Hispanic pupils in the U.S. It is suggested that, until these tests are normed and standardized on LEP and Hispanic pupils in the U.S., an armchair "scale of appropriateness" should be used to gauge the degree of confidence that can be ascribed to any scores derived from them. Table 2 presents such a "scale." It is not meant to provide absolute guidelines. In fact, it has no empirical basis. Its purpose is to offer broad suggestions for judging the propriety of using the Mexico City SOMPA tests.

The Bateria Woodcock Psico-educativa en Español (Woodcock, 1982). This is the most comprehensive battery of tests presently available for assessing Hispanic LEP children. It covers two broad areas of assessment, cognition and achievement, and yields 12 cluster scores. The tests and their clusters are presented in Table 3.

Language Proficiency Tests. These types of tests are not really new. They have been available for many years. Their use, however, has been mainly as screening instruments for deciding when a child should be designated as LEP or as English-proficient in order to provide or terminate *Lau*-mandated services (however these are interpreted in local school districts). Their use in special education assessment has been

---

*For information about these tests, contact Professor Jane R. Mercer, Sociology Department, University of California, Riverside, CA 92521.

Table 2
Dimensions to Consider in Gauging the Propriety of the
Mexico City SOMPA Tests for Use with Children in the U.S.

	Appropriate ⟶ Less Appropriate ⟶ Least Appropriate		
Appropriate	1. recently arrived from Mexico City public schools	6. attended Mexico City public schools in the past	11. parents educated in Mexico City; child LEP though born and educated in U.S.
	2. recently arrived from the public or private schools of Mexico	7. attended the public or private schools of Mexico in the past	12. parents educated in Mexico; child bilingual though born and educated in U.S.
Less Appropriate	3. recently arrived from Mexico with limited school experience	8. limited school experience in Mexico in the past	13. parents from Mexico but with limited education there; child primarily English speaking and educated in U.S.
	4. recently arrived from Latin America's urban schools	9. attended schools in Latin America in the past	14. parents educated in Latin America; child is primarily English speaking and educated in U.S.
Least Appropriate	5. recently arrived from Latin America with little school exposure	10. limited school exposure in Latin America in the past	15. parents had no formal education in Latin America; child primarily English speaking and educated in U.S.

Table 3
Subtests and Their Clusters in the
Bateria Woodcock Psico-educativa en Español

Subtests

---

1. Picture Vocabulary
   (Vocabulario sobre dibujos)
2. Spatial Relations
   (Relaciones espaciales)
3. Visual Auditory Learning
   (Aprendizaje visual-auditivo)
4. Quantitative Concepts
   (Conceptos cuantitativos)
5. Visual Matching (Pareo visual)
6. Antonyms-Synonyms
   (Antonimos-Sínonimos)
7. Analysis-Synthesis
   (Analysis-Sintesis)
8. Numbers Reversed
   (Inversión de números)
9. Concept Formation
   (Formación de conceptos)
10. Analogies (Analogias)

11. Letter-Word Identification
    (Identificación de letras
    y palabras)
12. Word Attack
    (Análisis de palabras)
13. Passage Comprehension
    (Comprensión de textos)
14. Calculation (Cálculo)
15. Applied Problems
    (Problemas aplicados)
16. Dictation (Dictado)
17. Proofing (Comprobación)
18. Punctuation and Capital-
    ization (Puntuación y empleo
    de letras mayusculas)
19. Spelling (Ortografía)
20. Usage (Concordancia)

Clusters

Cognition

Broad Cognitive Ability (Subtests:
1 through 10)

Short/Pre-school Form of Broad
Cognitive Ability (1–4)

Oral Language (1, 6, 10)

Reasoning (7, 9, 10)

Visual-Perceptual Speed (2, 5)

Reading Aptitude (3, 5, 6, 10)

Mathematics Aptitude (5, 6, 7, 9)

Aptitude for Written Language
(3, 5, 6, 10)

Achievement

Reading (11, 12, 13)

Mathematics (14, 15)

Written Language (16, 17)

(Basic) Skills in Reading, Math,
and Written Language (11, 15, 16)

minimal, even when state law mandates it (Figueroa, in press-a). Their importance in these types of assessments, however, is critical. Language is *the* covariate to consider and, where possible, to control with Hispanic pupils' testing.

In spite of the fact that there are many tests of Spanish and English language proficiency, three have been found by a committee of experts for the State of California to meet minimum technical standards (Merino & Spencer, 1983). These are: The Language Assessment Scales, Bilingual Syntax Measure, and the IDEA Proficiency Test.

The Language Assessment Scales (LAS; DeAvila & Duncan, 1975, 1977, 1981) are designed to measure oral language proficiency in English and Spanish. The LAS has some strengths as a language proficiency test that should be noted: (1) the materials were developed with the Hispanic population in mind; (2) the test attempts to tap more than one area of linguistic proficiency, i.e., syntax, phonology, vocabulary, and storytelling; (3) there seems to be a moderate relationship between the LAS and school achievement; (4) the LAS can be used with children representing a relatively wide age range; and (5) the developers provide descriptions of the different fluency levels: NES (non-English speaking), LES (limited English speaking), and FES (fluent English speaking).

The *Bilingual Syntax Measure I* (BSM I; Burt et al., 1976) is designed to assess English and Spanish oral language proficiency of students in grades kindergarten through second. Syntactic structures are elicited via questions asked of the students while looking at a series of pictures. The BSM is an attractive test that is easy to administer and score. Of the three language proficiency tests discussed here, the English version of the BSM I is the most solidly grounded on research concerning the acquisition of English as a second language.

The *IDEA Proficiency Test* (IPT; Dalton, 1979) is designed to measure vocabulary production, vocabulary comprehension, syntax, verbal expression, and articulation. Items vary widely. Students are asked alternately to respond to commands, identify pictures, repeat sentences, retell a short story, discriminate minimal sound pairs, describe an object, and select the main idea from a short passage. For a thorough, critical review of the IPT, readers are referred to McCollum (1983).

Other tests will be in use soon. The *Baja California SOMPA* tests, now in preparation, include all the tests originally developed in the California SOMPA. They are in this sense more complete than the Mexico City SOMPA. They may also be more relevant to Mexican children recently arrived in the United States insofar as the border region may be more similar to their background and experiences.

The Baja California SOMPA tests should be available in late 1984. Like all the previously mentioned tests, their appropriateness must be determined on an individual basis.

The English version of the *Kaufman Assessment Battery for Children* (K-ABC, Kaufman & Kaufman, 1983) has received wide press coverage. It purports to do nonbiased assessment in two ways. First, it separates the areas of assessment that are culturally loaded (and that were often included in verbal sections of tests such as the WISC-R and the Stanford-Binet) and aggregates these under one general, individually administered *achievement* set of subtests. The nonverbal subtests alone are considered cognitive tests. Second, it provides different norms for Black children in a manner analogous to Mercer's Estimated Learning Potential. This is done through percentile ranks for socioculturally different children.

The K-ABC is an extremely attractive test for young children (in fact, its baseline age is 2½). It seems to produce mean ethnic scores that are not as disparate as those procured with the WISC-R. The test is presently being touted as the possible replacement to the WISC-R.

The Present State of the Art

The testing abuses and misclassification of Hispanic children in special education gave rise to a profound anti-testing, anti-special-education sentiment among Hispanic professionals (e.g., Garcia, 1977). This is presently being tempered by the demographic explosion of the elementary school-age Hispanic and LEP population in the public schools, the clear emergence of a Hispanic handicapped population in the schools, and the appearance of a new field of study that has become known as bilingual special education. Within this new discipline, the area of testing has received a disproportionate amount of positive attention. Undoubtedly the progress made in developing Spanish language tests and the increase of bilingual testers has helped considerably in this regard. Also there is considerably more information on testing Hispanic children than on any other aspect of bilingual special education.

The following is a brief overview of some of the most critical areas to consider when testing Hispanic children. Where possible, data are also presented that have direct relevance to HHI and LEP/HHI children.

1. The heterogeneity of the Hispanic population is a critical consideration in testing. Not only are there extensive national, ethnic, and racial differences but there is also a wide range of Spanish/English

linguistic, dialectal, and communicative variation. Underestimation of actual ability is typical when a child who has been exposed to another language is tested in English (Figueroa, in press-b).

Transnationalism is a fact of life for many children. Unfortunately it often "causes" educational symptoms comparable to those of handicapped youngsters. Many other sociocultural conditions (Figueroa, 1978) create pseudo learning disabilities in Hispanic pupils that cannot be handled in either English special education programs or bilingual education programs. It is becoming increasingly obvious that for many Hispanic children referred for special education assessment, their past and present environments have to be assessed and diagnosed with the same care as their own functioning.

The impact of culture on tests of adaptive behavior used with bicultural populations remains unknown and may, in fact, be quite complex. Figures 1 and 2 are presented in this context for purely heuristic purposes. The data are taken from the SOMPA Hispanic sample's ABIC subtest scores broken down by home language (Figure 2), and from the subsample of children whose parents indicated in the SOMPA Health History Inventories that their children either wore a hearing aid or had had an operation in their ear (Figure 1), again broken down by home language. The graphs show that (1) there are twice as many children with hearing problems in the Spanish-speaking group; (2) the language-background factor has a more pronounced impact in the group with hearing problems (i.e., greater dispensation); and (3) the Self-Maintenance (S), Nonacademic School Roles (N), and Community (C) subscales of the ABIC discriminate most between the Spanish speaking and the English speaking in the group with hearing problems.

The data in Figures 1 and 2 clearly suggest that adaptive behavior as measured by the ABIC may not be insensitive to home language and may in fact be more sensitive to the interaction of audiological problems and home language background. Until more research in this area is available, adaptive behavior, like IQ, may have to rely far more on the tester's interpretive ability than on the standardized score.

2. Nonverbal IQ tests provide one of the most reliable means to measure Hispanic children's intelligence. Verbal IQ tests tend to significantly underestimate Hispanic children's intelligence and may, in fact, be psychometrically biased against them (Jensen, 1974). Combining verbal and nonverbal IQs or items (as in the Stanford-Binet) leads to an underestimation of Hispanic children's IQs.

Figures 1 and 2
Comparative ABIC and SOMPA Subtest Mean Scores

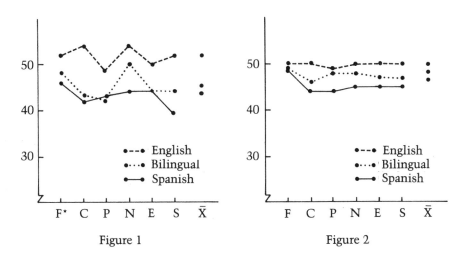

Figure 1   Figure 2

Note. ABIC subtest mean scores in hearing-impaired Hispanic children (Fig. 1) from Spanish-speaking (N = 20), bilingual (N = 8) and English-speaking (N = 8) homes compared to ABIC subtest mean scores of the Hispanic sample in SOMPA (Fig. 2) from Spanish-speaking (N = 221), bilingual (N = 204), and English-speaking (N = 265) homes.

*F = Family, C = Community, P = Peers, N = Nonacademic school roles, E = Earner/Consumer, S = Self-Maintenance.

As Figures 3, 4, and 5 show, subtest scores and IQ are markedly associated with language background. The more verbally and culturally loaded the test (e.g., Information, Similarities, Vocabulary, and Comprehension) the more that a Spanish-language background is related to lower scores.

3. The problems associated with assessing the language(s) of a child are exceedingly complex. Language proficiency tests are presently technically problematic. Procedures used in schools for determining the language of instruction are all too often devoid of reason. Economic factors tend to predominate in such decisions. Children are made academically retarded by a system that teaches in the

Figures 3, 4, and 5
Comparative WISC-R Subtest Mean Scores

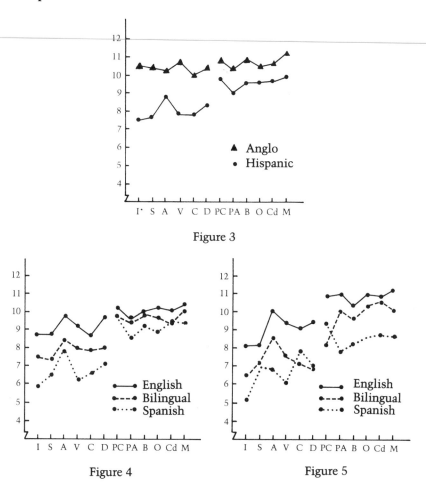

Figure 3

Figure 4   Figure 5

Note. SOMPA sample WISC-R subtest mean scores for (Fig. 3) Hispanic and Anglo children (N = 700 each group), (Fig. 4) three language groups of Hispanic children (N = 200 each group), and (Fig. 5) three language groups of Hispanic children with hearing problems (N = 17 Spanish, 8 bilingual, 8 English).

*I = Information, S = Similarities, A = Arithmetic, V = Vocabulary, C = Comprehension, D = Digit Span, PC = Picture Completion, PA = Picture Arrangement, B = Block Design, O = Object Assembly, Cd = Coding, M = Mazes.

wrong language; changes them to bilingual, to ESL, or to English-only programs from year to year; or provides "bilingual instruction" in English with a periodic translation given by a bilingual aide whose own educational background is marginal.

Extensive home and school observations have to be made to determine whether Spanish or English or both should be used in testing. The tester should be bilingual with a broad background in first and second language acquisition as well as dialect variants. The bilingual and bicultural skills of the tester are, for the present, the most critical and liable components in Hispanic testing.

4. The empirical literature has documented the existence of two ethnic patterns of mental abilities of Hispanic children that may directly or indirectly affect test outcomes. Ramirez and Castañeda (1974) made an elaborate case for bicultural sensitivity in education based on Mexican-American children's field-dependent learning styles (Witkin, 1962, 1977). This phenomenon has been documented in other Hispanic groups (Figueroa, 1980b; Holtzman et al., 1975; Kagan & Buriel, 1978). If, in fact, Hispanic children are more field-dependent, their nonverbal IQs may well be affected accordingly. The reason is that many nonverbal tests require "disembedding" skills that are more perceptual than cognitive and that are more typical of field-independents than field-dependents.

5. Since *Diana* in 1970, most court cases involving Hispanic testing have not been anti-testing. Accommodations to estabished procedures, such as using nonverbal intelligence tests, have been fairly typical. Such an "atmosphere" may have encouraged the development of Spanish versions of tests such as those in SOMPA and the Bateria Woodcock Psico-educativa. With the emergence of these instruments, the concerns about testing have focused on the competencies of the tester.

A side issue involves the use of interpreters in testing. Though the practice of using a native speaker to translate during testing is fairly widespread, it has received scant acknowledgment in the literature (Figueroa et al., in press). There are, regrettably, no studies on the impact of this practice on test validity.

6. If one follows a rigidly psychometric definition of bias (Cleary et al., 1975; Reynolds, 1982), there is little evidence that tests are biased against Hispanics (Sattler, 1982). This conclusion applies especially to studies involving prediction (to achievement, other test scores,

etc.) and internal test characteristics such as item difficulty levels and internal test reliabilities. These studies, however, may well prove to be naive (Figueroa, in press-b).

There is one aspect of test bias peculiar to LEP children that has not been investigated. This involves the popular practice of translating tests from English to Spanish and then using the English norms to produce a score. There is empirical evidence which shows that translating verbal test items does not automatically lead to translating the items' difficulty levels.

7. There is one inescapable fact about assessments of Hispanics: they are more time consuming and more expensive. They require more training and investment of money in Spanish language materials. Administrators need to realize this. The case load for a clinician who works with Hispanic children should reflect the extra effort and time required.

8. There is an urgent need for research and development in the entire matter of Hispanic assessment. Some of the available Spanish language instruments need to be studied and renormed with U.S. Hispanics. Their contribution to linguistically appropriate IEPs and instructional services also needs to be validated.

Diana Revisited

During the first six months of 1983, a team of investigators visited five school districts in California that had a history of EMR classes over-represented with Hispanic chidren. Figueroa (in press-a) had discovered that, according to data from the U.S. Office of Civil Rights, there were more districts in California overrepresented with Hispanic children in EMR classes than the state was actually reporting (as required under a 1974 federal court order). Visits to the five school districts indicated that, at least in those districts, most of the abuses described in the *Diana* complaint were still occurring. Other data (Twomey et al., 1980) suggest that these problems are generalizable to most school districts in California. Hispanic children are not being assessed in their native language. Language proficiency data are not being routinely used in assessment or placement decisions. Their culture and sociocultural background are not being considered. *Lau* is seldom taken into account in IEPs. Worst of all, the case studies of the Hispanic children placed in EMR classes strongly suggest that professional incompetence is not that infrequent. The California Rural Legal Assistance, counsel for the class of children represented in *Diana*, is actively considering pursuing a different legal tactic, i.e., professional malpractice.

Assessment of Hispanic/LEP Hearing Impaired

Throughout most of the material reviewed in this article, the term *hearing impaired* could easily have been substituted for *Hispanic*. The history of the assessment of hearing-impaired people shares a remarkable resemblance to that of Hispanic children. There is a tremendous heterogeneity in the population (Levine, 1981). Hearing-impaired people's IQs have the same classical PIQ-VIQ discrepancy (Ross, 1970). Whereas verbal IQs can fall well into the mentally retarded range, performance IQs and subtests are often in the average range (Schick, 1934; Mylebust & Burchard, 1945; Savage, 1979; Savage et al., 1981). The failure to account for the linguistic experience of the deaf has often led to a misdiagnosis of mental retardation (Lane, 1948). Discrimination in education and testing (as well as employment) is all too frequent (Levine, 1981). There are few clinicians capable of doing assessments with the hearing impaired (Levine, 1971, 1974). Verbal and performance tests have often been modified with predictably undesirable consequences, especially in "translations" of verbal instruments (Levine, 1981). Nonverbal tests can be more justifiably "adapted" insofar as interpreting *instructions* does not lead to changes in the test *items*.

Though some tests specifically normed and standardized on the hearing impaired are available, the majority of clinicians continue to use locally adapted versions of tests developed on hearing populations (Levine, 1981). Attempts to validate test results of deaf children using hearing-standardized tests have started to take into account adaptive behaviors outside formal learning environments (Levine, 1981). Recognition is finally being given to the unique environmental experiences of deaf children that attenuate their test results, such as lack of exposure to test materials, and home-school differences (Levine, 1981). Even the recommendations made in the Spartanburg conference (on the "Preparation of Psychological Service Providers to the Deaf;" Levine, 1977) apply with near-equal relevance to Hispanics.

The one area where the history of testing for the deaf does not co-incide with that for Hispanics is in the development of norms or tests that are specifically geared to meet the needs of limited English-proficient/Hispanic hearing-impaired (LEP/HHI) groups. There are tests for the hearing impaired (cf. Levine, 1981). There are none for LEP/HHI. It is quite likely, in fact, that the development of such instruments will have to wait on the development of U.S.-normed Spanish tests for LEP populations (covaried with Spanish/English levels of proficiency). For the present, as Zieziula (1982) has noted, only guidelines—gleaned from the history of Hispanic and hearing impaired assessment, together with adaptations of available Spanish and English tests—can be proposed.

Guidelines

1. Experienced educators of hearing-impaired children are only too familiar with the language acquisition difficulties imposed by auditory deficiencies. It is without question the number one educational problem with long-term consequences. There is increasing recognition that deaf children may well have "language" (simply defined as the ability and skill to express concepts and needs and the learned utilization of arbitrary symbols). However, not unlike Hispanics, hearing-impaired children and adults seldom reach a high level of fluency in the dominant language—English. Still, assessment of intelligence, academic achievement, class placement, etc., are very closely related to language mastery. It is not known how many HHI have sufficient hearing to benefit from oral/aural input, but when there is some hearing and the dominant language in the home is not English, bilingualism must be a consideration. And to be considered, this bilingualism needs to be assessed.

   The technology and competencies needed for doing this type of assessment of "bilingual communicative competence" waits for research and development. Until such data and validated procedures are available, the best course of action for the clinician is to undertake observational study of the child's daily communicative pattern in the home, neighborhood, and school (in that order of priority). Assuming that the clinician has a high level of Spanish/English proficiency, this type of investigation should yield a fairly accurate picture of the child's present functioning in one or both languages in various domains and also of the language preferences and proficiency of the child's support systems.

As a follow up to this process, language proficiency tests should be administered whenever more discrete (and hence more complete) information is needed for remediation/teaching purposes. Of the three language proficiency tests reviewed previously, the IPT may offer the best means for doing this type of assessment with LEP/HHI. The BSM is clearly too problematic in that it relies on syntactical structures to gauge language proficiency. English syntax is one of the most difficult linguistic skills for the hearing impaired (Levine, 1981) and may therefore contaminate any language proficiency score derived from the BSM. Tests that look at several parameters of language proficiency will better enable a hearing-impaired student to demonstrate her/his linguistic and communicative competence.

2. Everything that applies to the evaluation of a Hispanic child's life experience (migration, social units, educational age, etc.) applies to LEP/HHI. An extremely useful test for measuring a Hispanic family's distance from an Anglo, middle class family's sociocultural characteristics is the SOMPA Sociocultural Scales and their Anglo norms. These will easily provide the tester with critical information about the degree of testing effort that should be spent in order to limit any cultural bias, and about the likelihood that any U.S. norms will invalidly evaluate an individual from that family. The more distance between a family's background and that of U.S. middle class society, the more cautiously should a tester proceed.

3. Translation of verbal test items, be it to the child's preferred mode of communication or home language, almost always involves the creation of a new test, one whose properties remain unknown and may in fact be invalid. Nonverbal tests, subtests, and items are not as susceptible to these problems. Whenever instruction of nonverbal tests are translated or interpreted, two important precautions should be taken: (a) ensure that the *instructions* to these tests are age-appropriate and accurate across languages and modes of communication, and (b) determine whether the norms of such tests do not systematically lead to lower or higher scores for Hispanic clients. If norms do systematically lead to lower or higher scores, the clinician must determine whether such disparities are unacceptably large or small enough to be managed by conservative and cautious diagnostic inferences.

4. It is better to do an in-depth case study of an individual HHI/LEP child than to rely on questionable psychometric procedures. Tests

are essentially an economic way of judging an individual's functioning. The same data can be gathered through less economical observational and longitudinal procedures provided the examiner knows the contextual parameters in which cognitive, linguistic, communicative, affective, and academic development occurred. Unacculturated clinicians are as bad as culturally inappropriate tests. The tester of HHI/LEP pupils must be knowledgeable about Hispanic culture and language, about hearing impaired testing, and about instruments and procedures available for diagnostic work with HHI/LEP individuals.

5. If an individual is appropriately tested in her/his language and mode of communication, she/he should be taught in a similarly appropriate language and mode of communication. As with Hispanic children's education, the education of HHI/LEP pupils has often been less than meaningful or humane. There are many instances where HHI/LEP children have been communicatively separated from their parents because signing and instruction were taught in English. *Lau* is more relevant for HHI/LEP children than for normal-hearing children if one takes into account the extended didactic roles that parents of the hearing impaired undertake in raising their offspring. Linguistically appropriate testing should lead to linguistically appropriate teaching.

6. Levine (1974) conducted a survey of testers who work with the hearing impaired. A list of the most commonly used cognitive, personality, and achievement English tests for the hearing impaired was presented in that study. The left column of Table 4 presents a shortened version of Levine's list. The right column presents the Spanish equivalents of these tests as well as those nonverbal tests that can be used with HHI/LEP (provided their instructions are translated appropriately; cf. 3 above). Other Spanish language tests are also listed. Levine's list includes those tests specifically developed and normed for the hearing impaired. Such tests are not available for HHI/LEP. Should any such tests ever be contemplated, consideration should be given to controlling for the interactions of language, culture, and hearing loss. Procedures such as the SOMPA Estimated Learning Potential or the K-ABC sociocultural norms may well be needed.

The Leiter, WAIS-R Performance, Goodenough-Harris, WPPSI Performance, Columbia, Ravens, and Draw-a-Person will, in all likelihood, lead to lower scores for Hispanic children. The precautions listed above (cf. 3) should be followed.

Table 4
The Most Commonly Used Tests with Hearing-Impaired Clients
and Comparable Spanish Language Tests for Use with HHI

English	Spanish
Cognition	

A. WISC-R Performance	WISC-R Performance*
	 —U.S. norms
	 —Mexico City norms/
	    instructions
	 —Baja California norms/
	    instructions

B. Leiter	Leiter*
C. WAIS Performance	WAIS-R Performance*
D. Hiskey-Nebraska Test of Learning Aptitude	
E. Goodenough-Harris	Goodenough-Harris*
F. WPPSI-Performance	WPPSI-Performance*
G. Arthur Adaptation of the Leiter	Arthur Adaptation of the Leiter*
H. Columbia Mental Maturity Scale	Columbia Mental Maturity Scale*
I. Merrill-Palmer Scale of Mental Tests	Merrill-Palmer Scale of Mental Tests*
J. Ravens Progressive Matrices	Ravens Progressive Matrices*
K. Ontario School Ability Examination	
L. Stanford-Binet	
Personality	
A. Bender Gestalt	SOMPA Bender, Mexico City SOMPA Bender, Baja California SOMPA Bender (norms available for the Bender as a test for visual- motor integration)
B. Draw-a-Person	
C. House-Tree-Person	
D. TAT	
E. Rorschach	

continued

Table 4

Personality continued

F. Vineland Social Maturity Scale	Vineland Social Maturity Scale*
G. Rotter Incomplete Sentences	Rotter Incomplete Sentences* SOMPA validation translation (Figueroa & Sassenrath, 1984); SOMPA ABIC (U.S., Mexico City, and Baja California norms)

Achievement

A. WRAT	Bateria Woodcock Psico-educativa, Mexico City K-ABC,
B. Stanford Achievement	Comprehensive Tests of Basic
C. Metropolitan Achievement	Skills-Spanish, Prueba Boehm de
D. Gates Reading Achievement	Conceptos Basicos, California Achievement Tests-Spanish,
E. California Achievement	Cooperative Preschool Inventory-Spanish Edition.

*Carefully translated instructions, U.S. norms used with precautions previously noted.

7. Ideally, the following assessment sequence should be considered when testing an HHI/LEP child. First, an accurate determination must be made of the degree of hearing loss. It is quite possible that any audiological examination can be seriously compromised if the instructions are not conveyed in the language or mode of communication most familiar to the child. Whenever possible, this should be checked and ruled out. Second, the predominant language system should be determined. Testing should be done using the language that is clearly the strongest or using both of the child's languages. Third, a measure of English/Spanish language proficiency should be taken. Fourth, the child's background and transcultural experiences should be determined, paying particular attention to the distance between these and the Anglo, middle class expectations of the U.S. educational system (regular or special education). Fifth, a determination should be made as to the cross-cultural capabilities of the client. This requires an assessment of the individual's functioning in the

home/cultural environment and in the school/U.S. environment. Sixth, educational interventions should be developed that are linguistically appropriate.

Discussion

Research and practice in measurement of hearing-impaired people and Hispanics share common areas of concern: linguistic emphasis (dominant language acquisition), interpreters/translators, performance/nonverbal emphasis, and administrator competency, to name a few.

Review of the literature seems to verify that in the area of bilingual education more advances have been made in research, selection, and utilization of measurement instruments than in education of the deaf.

Data continue to emerge related to achievement and behaviors indicating that, within the national population of deaf children, Hispanic and other minority children (1) score lower in intelligence and achievement tests, (2) are identified more often as multihandicapped, and (3) have a higher prevalence of emotional/behavioral problems.

Overall intelligence of deaf students on nonverbal scales is comparable to hearing students. This is also true of Hispanic and non-Hispanic students.

It appears, then, that the differences and deficiencies of these groups are for the most part attributable to linguistic and communication problems which they share in somewhat different ways.

Until there are tests normed and standardized on HHI and HHI/LEP populations, the *tester* must seek to meet the unique needs of such a population. The tester's language and communication skills, as well as his/her cross-cultural skills, are singularly critical. The history of Hispanic testing as well as the recent development of Spanish language tests are cause for both caution and optimism.

There is urgent need to begin to gather comparative data on these populations. There is much need for dialogue between the measurement professionals who work with the Hispanic and the hearing impaired. There are some beginnings in special education, but forums are needed to discuss, assess, and implement the findings and contributions of both fields.

References

Blackhurst, A. E., & Berdine, W. H. (Eds.). *An introduction to special education.* Boston: Little, Brown, 1981.

Burt, M., Dulay, H., & Hernandez-Chavez, E. *Bilingual syntax measure.* San Francisco: Harcourt, Brace, Jovanovich, 1976.

Cleary, T. A., Humphreys, L. G., Kendrick, S. A., & Wesman, A. Educational uses of tests with disadvantaged students. *American Psychologist,* 1975, *15,* 15–40.

Coulter, A., & Morrow, H. *The concept and measurement of adaptive behavior.* New York: Grune & Stratton, 1978.

Dalton, E. F. *IDEA Proficiency Test: Technical manual.* Whittier, Calif.: Ballard & Tighe, 1979.

Dean, R. S. Analysis of the PIAT with Anglo and Mexican American children. *Journal of School Psychology,* 1977, *15,* 329–333. (a)

Dean, R. S. Internal consistency of the PIAT with Mexican American children. *Psychology in the Schools,* 1977, *14,* 167–168. (b)

Dean, R. S. Predictive validity of the WISC-R with Mexican American children. *Journal of School Psychology,* 1979, *17,* 55–58.

DeAvila, E., & Duncan, S. *Language assessment scales I and II.* San Rafael, Calif.: Linguametrics Group, 1975, 1977, 1981.

DeBlassie, R. R. *Testing Mexican American youth.* Hingham, Mass.: Teaching Resources, 1980.

Diana v. California State Board of Education. C-70 37, District Court of Northern California, February 1970.

Dirección General de Educación Especial. *SOMPA sistema de evaluacion multicultural y pluralistico: Manual de calificacion.* Mexico, D.F.: Graficas Corona, 1982.

Figueroa, R. A. Individualizing instruction in the bilingual classroom. *The Bilingual Review/La Revista Bilingue,* 1978, *5,* 48–56.

Figueroa, R. A. The Adaptive Behavior Inventory for Children. Paper presented at the 88th Annual Convention of the American Psychological Association, Montreal, September 1980. (a)

Figueroa, R. A. Field dependence, ethnicity, and cognitive styles. *Hispanic Journal of Behavioral Sciences,* 1980, *2,* 35–42. (b)

Figueroa, R. A. *Diana revisited.* Los Angeles: National Dissemination and Assessment Center, in press-a.

Figueroa, R. A. Test bias and Hispanic children. *Journal of Special Education,* in press-b.

Figueroa, R. A., Sandoval, J., & Merino, B. School psychology and limited-English-proficient (LEP) children: New competencies. *Journal of School Psychology,* in press.

Garcia, J. Intelligence testing: Quotients, quotas, and quackery. In J. L. Martinez (Ed.), *Chicano psychology.* New York: Academic Press, 1977.

Gomez-Palacio, M., Padilla, E., & Roll, S. *WISC-R Mexicano.* Mexico, D.F.: Foto Composición Reyes, 1982.

Gomez-Palacio, M., Rangel-Hinojosa, E., & Padilla, E. *Estandarización de la bateria de pruebas SOMPA en Mexico, D. F.* Mexico, D. F.: Secretaría de Educación Publica para la Dirección General de Educacion Especial, 1982.

Heber, R. A manual on terminology and classification in mental retardation. *American Journal of Mental Deficiency,* Monograph Supplement, 1981.

Holtzman, W. H., Diaz-Guerrero, R., & Swartz, J. D. *Personality development in two cultures.* Austin: University of Texas Press, 1975.

Jensen, A. R. How biased are culture loaded tests? *Genetic Psychology Monographs,* 1974, *90,* 185–244.

Kagan, S., & Buriel, R. Field dependence-independence and Mexican American culture and education. In J. L. Martinez (Ed.), *Chicano psychology.* New York: Academic Press, 1978.

Kaufman, A. S., & Kaufman, N. L. *K-ABC Kaufman Assessment Battery for Children.* Circle Pines, Minn.: American Guidance Service, 1983.

Lane, H. S. Some psychological problems involved in working with the deaf and hard of hearing. *Journal of Rehabilitation,* 1948, *14,* 24–29.

Lau v. Nichols. United States Supreme Court. 414 U.S. 563 (1974).

Levine, E. S. Mental measurement of the deaf child. *Volta Review,* 1971, *73,* 80–104.

Levine, E. S. Psychological tests and practices with the deaf: A survey of the state of the art. *Volta Review,* 1974, *76,* 298–319.

Levine, E. S. *The preparation of psychological service providers to the deaf* (PRWAD Monograph No. 4). Silver Spring, Md.: *Journal of Rehabilitation of the Deaf,* 1977.

Levine, E. S. *The ecology of early deafness.* New York: Columbia University Press, 1981.

McCollum, P. A. The IDEA Oral Language Proficiency Test: A critical review. In S. S. Seider & V.A. Rosslyn (Eds.), *Issues of language assessment: V. II: Language assessment and curriculum planning.* Dallas: National Clearinghouse on Bilingual Education (Evaluation, Dissemination, and Assessment Center), 1983.

Mercer, J. R. IQ: The lethal label. *Psychology Today,* September 1972, 44–47, 95–97.

Mercer, J. R. *Labeling the mentally retarded.* Berkeley: University of California Press, 1973.

Mercer, J. R., & Lewis, J. F. *The system of multicultural pluralistic assessment: Conceptual and technical manual.* New York: Psychological Corporation, 1979.

Merino, B. J., & Spencer, M. The comparability of English and Spanish versions of oral language proficiency instruments. *NABE Journal,* 1983, 7, 1–31.

Myklebust, H. R., & Burchard, E. M. L. A study of the effects of congenital and adventitious deafness on the intelligence, personality, and social maturity of school children. *Journal of Educational Psychology,* 1945, 36, 321–343.

Padilla, A. M., & Ruiz, R. A. *Latino mental health: A review of the literature.* Rockville, Md.: National Institute of Mental Health, 1973.

Pletcher, B. P., Locks, N. A., Reynolds, D. F., & Sisson, B. G. *A guide to assessment instruments for limited English-speaking students.* New York: Santillana, 1978.

Ramirez, M., & Castañeda, A. *Cultural democracy, bicognitive development, and education.* New York: Academic Press, 1974.

Reschly, D. J. Assessing mild mental retardation: The influence of adaptive behavior, sociocultural status, and prospects for nonbiased assessment. In C. R. Reynolds and T. B. Gutkin (Eds.), *The handbook of school psychology.* New York: Wiley & Sons, 1982.

Reynolds, C. R. The problem of bias in psychological assessment. In C. R. Reynolds & T. B. Gutkin (Eds.), *The handbook of school psychology.* New York: Wiley & Sons, 1982.

Ross, D. R. A technique of verbal ability assessment of deaf adults. *Journal of Rehabilitation of the Deaf,* 1970, 3, 7–15.

Samuda, R. J. *Psychological testing of American minorities: Issues and consequences.* New York: Dodd, Mead & Co., 1975.

Sanchez, G. I. Group differences in Spanish-speaking children: A critical review. *Journal of Applied Psychology,* 1932, *16,* 549–558. (a)

Sanchez, G. I. Scores of Spanish-speaking children on repeated tests. *Journal of Genetic Psychology,* 1932, *40,* 223–231. (b)

Sanchez, G. I. Bilingualism and mental measures: A word of caution. *Journal of Applied Psychology,* 1934, *18,* 765–772.

Sattler, J. M. *Assessment of children's intelligence and special abilities.* Boston: Allyn & Bacon, 1982.

Savage, J. F. The measurement and structure of perceptual-motor functioning and its relationship to reading achievement in normal and hearing-impaired children. Unpublished doctoral dissertation, University of Newcastle upon Tyne, 1979.

Savage, R. D., Evans, L., & Savage, J. F. *Psychology and communication in deaf children.* Sydney: Grune & Stratton, 1981.

Schick, H. F. A performance for deaf children of school age. *Volta Review,* 1934, *34,* 657–665.

Subsecretaria de Educación Elemental, Dirección General de Educación Especial. *SOMPA sistema de evaluación multicultural y pluralistico: Manual de aplicación.* Mexico, D.F.: Litográfica Osa Mayor, 1982.

Twomey, S. C., Gallegos, C., Andersen, L., Williamson, B., & Williamson, J. *A study of the effectiveness of various nondiscriminatory and linguistically and culturally appropriate assessment criteria for placement of minority students in special education programs.* Merced, Calif.: Planning Associates, 1980.

United States Commission on Civil Rights. *The unfinished education: Report II, Mexican American educational study.* Washington, D.C.: U.S. Government Printing Office, 1971.

United States Commission on Civil Rights. *Toward quality education for Mexican Americans: Report VI, Mexican American education study.* Washington, D.C.: U.S. Government Printing Office, 1974.

Waggoner, D. Non-English language background persons: Three U.S. surveys. *TESOL Quarterly,* 1978, *12,* 247–253.

Witkin, H. A., Dyk, R. B., Faterson, H. F., Goodenough, D. R., & Karp, S. A. *Psychological differentiation.* New York: Wiley, 1962.

Witkin, H. A., Moore, C. A., Goodenough, D. R., & Cox, P. W. Field dependent and field independent cognitive styles and their educational implications. *Review of Educational Research,* 1977, *47,* 1–64.

Woodcock, R. W. *Examiners manual: Bateria Woodcock Psico-educativa en Español.* Hingham, Mass.: Teaching Resources, 1982.

Zieziula, F. R. *Assessment of hearing-impaired people.* Washington, D.C.: Gallaudet College Press, 1982.

Educational Programming

11

Issues in the Development of Culturally Responsive Programs for Deaf Students from Non-English-Speaking Homes

Peter M. Blackwell and Joseph E. Fischgrund

During a parent meeting at the Rhode Island School for the Deaf, the mother of one student asked, "Does Ricardo know he is Portuguese?" The question dramatized the need for programs for the deaf that are responsive to students' home language and culture. Deaf students with non-English-speaking parents historically have not had access to the special education systems developed for the deaf and hearing impaired. And, except for some recently developed approaches, educators of the deaf and hearing impaired have made little or no effort to adapt to the needs of a culturally diverse population.

Responding to the cultural diversity within its own population, the Rhode Island School for the Deaf (RISD) initiated bilingual/bicultural services in 1976. These initial efforts soon expanded and formed the basis for what is now Projecto Oportunidad, a Title VII Demonstration Project in the bilingual/bicultural education of the hearing impaired. This program currently provides a full range of services—educational services including instruction in Spanish, Portuguese, and Chinese; counseling and social services for families; a sign language class for Spanish-speaking parents; and multicultural resource services to other programs for the hearing impaired.

The linguistic issues relating directly to language choice or mode use for hearing-impaired students whose home language is other than English have been addressed in detail elsewhere (see chapters 7 and 8). Equally important are issues centering on the role of culture in the child/family/school relationship. In the following sections, we discuss some specific aspects of these issues.

Issues Relating to the Child

A. Etiology

It is important to recognize initially that the causes of deafness in children from diverse countries may be very different from the causes of deafness in the rest of the school population. For example, the educational system for hearing-impaired children in the United States has focused on the concentration of rubella deafness. For Azorean (Portuguese) children in the same age group at RISD, however, the primary cause of deafness was meningitis. While nearly all of their U.S.-born classmates were congenitally deaf, the Azorean children had acquired their deafness between the ages of 2 and 11. In a study of deaf children in New York City programs for the hearing impaired, Lerman and Cortez (1977) found that 30 percent of the Hispanic deaf students were postlingually deaf compared with only 22 percent of the non-Hispanic deaf population. These differences must be considered in developing an educational plan that truly matches a child's abilities.

B. Identification

Hearing impairment is generally identified later in children from non-English-speaking (NES) homes than in children from English-speaking homes. A survey of RISD students showed that children from immigrant, NES families were identified as hearing impaired and fitted with hearing aids significantly later than their peers from English-speaking families. Some of this may be due to the fact that more of the latter children were congenitally deaf. The difference is more adequately explained, however, by variables such as rural/urban, parent age, parent educational level, availability of medical services, etc.

When the child of an immigrant family is identified in the U.S. as hearing impaired, it is important that a culturally appropriate person and setting be utilized in discussing that identification. The bicultural personnel at RISD do more than just explain the deafness to the family in its native language; they also provide a buffer between the family and the alien culture while family members struggle to come to terms with the child's handicap.

C. Early Intervention, Assessment, and Training

Early intervention with the hearing-impaired child is best accomplished by professional staff who are linguistically and culturally appropriate. Interpreters may serve useful functions in some contexts, but their use in situations such as parent counseling, parent training, or home visits is not recommended. Hispanic families prefer to relate on a personal basis with the person who is intervening on behalf of their child, even when that person is representing an agency or school. Once a trusting relationship has been established, this person becomes the family's primary reference point and information source for almost anything having to do with the hearing-impaired child. If the early intervention is to have any impact at all, every effort should be made to find culturally and linguistically appropriate professional personnel for initial and ongoing contacts with NES families.

For example, the need for early and consistent amplification for the hearing-impaired child is very often not understood by NES parents. This happens not because there is no way to discuss hearing aids in Spanish, but because the use of amplification devices may have been quite uncommon in the parents' home culture. While amplification is important to the interventionist, it may not be a high priority for the family that is struggling for the basic necessities of life. One can expect some delays in properly fitting the child with hearing aids, especially if social service agencies are involved. Professionals often express their dismay and anger at families for missing appointments or not following up on hearing-aid acquisition and maintenance. This however is more often due to lack of understanding than lack of caring by the parents. A primary function of the bilingual/bicultural program is to provide a framework within which the family can comfortably understand and begin to meet the demands of the hearing-impaired child and of the system that seeks to assist that child.

Another important role of the bilingual/bicultural program is that it works with parents on communication skills with their deaf child. This is done in the language of the parents while introducing them to the English speaking and signing environment of the school. The all-too-common practice of asking parents to speak to their child in English is ill-advised because it is detrimental to parent-child interaction; it can only make the parents feel inadequate at a time when they are just beginning to deal with the child's deafness. Interaction is the most important aspect of early language development. Therefore, it is important that NES parents not be made to feel even more distant from their deaf child because of their inability to speak or sign English. Through utilization of bilingual/bicultural personnel, a truly total communication approach to early intervention can be utilized with deaf children from NES homes.

Issues Relating to the Families

Any successful bilingual/bicultural program must address the sociocultural status of students' families. This is no less the case for hearing-impaired students, particularly since the roots of language development and social understanding and conduct are in family interaction. Deaf as well as hearing children receive their first exposure to language and its social accompaniments in the family setting. This exposure is often more important for hearing-impaired students from other countries and cultures than for similar children on the U.S. mainland. The foreign-born children often enter the U.S. with little or no prior educational experience and, in many cases, no exposure to other hearing-impaired individuals. For example, Hispanic students coming to the U.S. from Latin American countries or to the mainland from Puerto Rico very likely were not involved in special education programs. Therefore, family interaction may be their only social and linguistic experience. In order to properly assess and fully understand these students, it is necessary to understand their families in an historical, social, and cultural context.

An example of this is found in an excellent study of Puerto Rican families living on the U.S. mainland. Figler (1981) described some remarkable trends in Puerto Rican families with handicapped children compared to those without. As one might expect, the families with handicapped children experienced greater difficulty with housing, jobs, agency contact, and other practical issues. What was unexpected was the change in attitudes central to their cultural and emotional base. Most Puerto Rican families have a continuing desire to return to the island, a feeling that provides strength for the family. But families of handicapped children did not express this desire as strongly; the presence of the handicap and the lack of special educational services on the island tend to exclude them from the dream and cycle of return.

Understanding aspects of the families' cultural responses to their current situations, like the example cited above, is the first step in working successfully with these families. It is also a prerequisite to any kind of parent training activities.

Arredondo-Dowd (1981) described immigrant families' reactions to their displacement as part of a grieving process not unlike responses to death (Kubler-Ross, 1969). The grieving process has other parallels in the paradigm, outlined by Luterman (1978), describing parents' responses to the discovery of deafness in their child. Understanding this matrix of responses would be important in working with a Puerto Rican family that has learned that their child is deaf.

As Figler (1982) stated so well, "what are strengths for the family when they get on the plane in San Juan are perceived as negatives when they get off the plane in New York." Among these strengths are family structure, religious belief system, community support system, and cultural value system (Delgado & Humm-Delgado, 1982). The role of the bilingual/bicultural program is to understand and utilize these strengths.

Issues Relating to School

A. Responding to the Demands of School

Many children from NES homes have had little or no educational experience prior to their entry into the mainland U.S. special educational system. Many of the Hispanic children entering schools for the deaf in the eastern part of the U.S.—even those enrolling as adolescents—have never been in school before. Therefore, the general demands of school—conventional learning behaviors, regular attendance, homework, the whole notion of parent involvement, the IEP process—are simply unfamiliar to both parent and child. This must be taken into account in the assessment and placement process; if not, misplacement and misdiagnosis of deaf children from NES homes will continue at its current alarming rate (Delgado, 1981).

Once the child is in school, it is not uncommon to find teachers and aides with well-intentioned concern about poor attendance, lack of parent response to school notices, and failure to reinforce school skills. The concern, however, often ends up as inadvertent criticism of students and parents for not understanding things with which they are basically unfamiliar. This may become the source of negative feelings between the educational institution on the one hand and the students and parents on the other.

Situations such as this provide one important reason for the establishment of bilingual/bicultural services. Specific programs are developed to help bridge any gaps between the demands of schooling and the perceptions and feelings of culturally diverse families. These programs are important to the deaf child throughout the assessment, placement, and school adjustment process. The cultural and linguistic mismatch between many Hispanic students and the curriculum which confronts them in school must be understood and accepted. This is the first step in the development of the bilingual/bicultural curriculum geared to students' linguistic, cognitive, social, and educational needs.

B. Choice of Languages

Having discussed many of the issues relating to the cultural status of the family and child, there remains the question of language choice. This issue is best approached by looking at the linguistic environments in which the hearing-impaired child participates. First, there is the language of the home; if this language is Spanish, the child is part of the Spanish linguistic community and context, no matter how profound the hearing impairment. This fact alone argues for some degree of bilingual instruction that will provide the student with links between his or her home and school languages. The range of such instruction is from direct teaching of oral Spanish to the use of a manual mode. For the child who becomes sign-language dominant through the school experience, there must be a program for both student and parent that bridges the child's sign language competence and the parents' home language.

A third fact of the child's linguistic environment, in addition to oral Spanish and a sign system, is the presence and role of English. For the hearing-impaired student who is dominant in Spanish, instruction in English as a second language (ESL) will need to be included in the language program. The ESL activities are distinct from the kind of language activities utilized to develop language in congenitally deaf students from English-speaking homes.

There may also be a need for continued developmental work in the home language, both for its own intrinsic communicative value and so that an adequate base for the acquisition of English skills is established (see chapter 8 for a complete discussion of these issues). There are statements to the effect that deaf children become confused by the use of different languages in their educational program. Such statements simply do not take into account the linguistic facts of life; in fact, they deny one facet of the children's being—their home language and culture. By recognizing and utilizing the linguistic diversity that exists in the deaf child's various environments, the bilingual/bicultural program clarifies the uses of the different languages and gives them positive, practical value.

C. Implementing a Bilingual/Bicultural Program in a School for the Deaf

Prior to the establishment of bilingual/bicultural services at RISD, the arrival of a deaf student from the Dominican Republic was announced at a school faculty meeting. The student was an 11-year-old girl who had never attended school. Immediately, questions related to class placement and, more critically, to what she should be taught were raised by the diagnostic and teaching staff. Units of study in the RISD curriculum about the Middle Ages, the feudal system, and Shakespeare certainly seemed inappropriate for this student. There was also considerable concern about how much English (in any mode) she would need before she could function in a regular classroom of deaf children.

The questions raised and answers provided then were—and still are—typical responses to the challenge of educating hearing-impaired children from limited English-speaking homes. Here is a summary of the questions and recommendations at that time:

1. What are the reasonable expectations for a child this age who has "no language"?

2. Because deaf children have so much difficulty in the acquisition of one language, would not the acquisition of two languages be inordinately difficult?

3. Given that two languages are out of the question and that this is an English-speaking society, shouldn't our efforts to teach the child English include discouraging the use of Spanish?

4. As the goal will be to develop English, we should ask the parents to speak English at home, especially to their deaf daughter; we do not want the use of Spanish in the home to confuse her and hinder her acquisition of English.

5. In the matter of language curriculum, we certainly must begin by working on the English vocabulary for things already familiar to the child—food, clothing, body parts, furniture, rooms in the house.

6. Because this child is 11, has had no formal education, and will soon enter adolescence, her program should contain only a minimum of academics. A minimal basic skills program should be provided until she is old enough to be in a vocational training program that includes a life-skills component.

These questions and recommendations were well-motivated. The conclusions seemed logical, in the best interests of the child, and within the capacity of the school to provide.

Ethnic and racial bias are often a contributing factor in such a decision-making process, but the responses described above are also a product of our experiences with an essentially monocultural population of deaf students, the desire to have our programs work for every child in the same way, and the general over-protectiveness of the education of the deaf. However well-motivated this thinking might be, it nevertheless indicates considerable misunderstanding of the language acquisition process, the nature of bilingualism, and the role of culture in the learning process and curriculum. The result of this misunderstanding is often misplacement and inappropriate programming for the hearing-impaired child from a different linguistic and cultural background. This is an old pattern that, unfortunately, persists today throughout education of the hearing impaired.

Today, with the experience of providing bilingual/bicultural services for nearly 10 years, RISD responds differently upon the arrival of deaf students like the girl from the Dominican Republic. Point by point, here are the bases for our response to similar students today:

1. Children who have had no formal education—particularly if they have no identifiable, conventional communication system such as speech or sign language—may appear to have "no language"; if the children also come from limited English-speaking homes, the likelihood of this conclusion is increased. In fact, linguistically and culturally appropriate personnel, utilizing similarly appropriate formats for evaluation, know otherwise. The bilingual/bicultural staff at RISD has never evaluated a hearing-impaired child, not otherwise handicapped, who has "no language." For some students there may not be a formal identifiable system, either oral or in sign. If language is understood in its primary and richest sense, however, it is possible to identify linguistic strategies that children are using to interact. When properly assessed by a person native to their culture and language, even students with profound hearing losses often indicate some degree of competence in the oral language of their culture (or sign system if they have been exposed to it).

2. The acquisition of English language skills can be a complex and difficult process for the hearing-impaired child. It is not necessarily true, however, that the involvement of a second language makes the process much more difficult. Although many U.S. citizens find it difficult to believe, bilingualism is as natural a linguistic and social phenomenon as monolingualism. Therefore a bilingual program should be a real consideration.

3. It appears to be a fact that the language of the home will continue to be part of the child's life; it will not go away simply because the school chooses to discourage or ignore it. The attempt to discourage the child's use of Spanish will only cause negative feelings and most likely will work to the child's disadvantage in the acquisition of English. In fact, the school should utilize the presence of the home language as a positive factor and provide some degree of instruction in that language.

4. Dubious assumptions are inherent in the view of language acquisition that suggests that, if the parents learn English and do not speak Spanish in the home, the hearing-impaired child will learn English better. Aside from that, the practical matter is that parents' motivation for learning English depends upon a complex set of factors. Even if they were motivated to learn English, their use of English would continue to be hesitant for some time and may provide an irrelevant language model for their hearing-impaired child. It is not the presence of a second language that confuses deaf children but rather their lack of awareness that two languages are involved in their lives and their not knowing when a particular language is being or should be used. Distorting parent-child interaction for the sake of minimal linguistic input appears to be a poor trade-off indeed.

5. The temptation to begin a language program by using vocabulary familiar to the child is understandable. The problem is that the content may be so familiar that new learning does not take place. One adolescent student entering RISD had been essentially homebound in her country of origin, cooking and doing housework. The English tutors chose cooking utensils as the content for language lessons, assuming that the student would quickly acquire the English names for them. As she was shown each item, however, the student only smiled broadly and indicated that indeed she knew what it was and how it was to be used. Unfortunately, she did not care to be taught what she already knew, and she became

increasingly frustrated with her tutors. The vocabulary lesson had no generalizable positive effects on her acquisition of a linguistic system.

Jerome Bruner (1973) described people whose "environment is banal in the sense of containing only high-probability events or, more properly, events and sequences that are strongly expected...as rigid or stuck" (p. 33). What seems to be needed in the curriculum is a balance between the familiar (so that there is a basis of knowledge) and the unfamiliar (so a need state [op. cit., p. 227] is created) that motivates categorization and symbolization through comparison and contrast.

6. There is no question that some degree of career or vocational education should be offered to the late beginner. But any precipitous assignment to a vocational program, especially if its goal is primarily life-skills training, often has the appearance of warehousing—of placing the student in the program not because it is the best choice but because no other curricular approach is available. This happens even in situations where the child has the ability to deal with a much wider range of subject matter.

What are the possibilities of meaningful programming for the kind of student described above? Adopting a developmental approach, it was decided that what was really needed was to establish a system of categorization upon which a linguistic system could be built. If this assumption was true, then the actual content of the teaching unit became somewhat arbitrary, as long as it was a conceptually based approach to the material and was socially and culturally responsive to the child's needs. If the child was to be placed in a regular (school for the deaf) classroom, he or she needed to internalize grammar at the simple sentence level while the other students were at a complex level. In practice this meant having the teacher introduce the ideas or concepts (feudal system, castle life, serfs) to the class as a whole; those ideas were then represented in complex sentences for students at that level and in simple sentences for the new students.

While this required more preparation by the teacher, it kept the class together for much of the day and allowed the new student to feel integral to the class. The unit of study on the Middle Ages was so new and different that the student, rather than being confused by that culture or by the language of the school, was highly motivated by the content. Moreover, in studying the various life-styles of people in the

Middle Ages there was much that the student could identify with—farming, food preparation, poverty—in ways that few of the other students could match.

In the section on curriculum planning for the late beginner in sentences and other systems (Blackwell et al., 1978), a teacher summarizes a more specific process of planning for students who begin their education late. The steps include:

1. The choice of high-interest content as an educational vehicle.

2. The representation of the new material in ways that establish a simple syntactic grammar utilizing basic semantic relationships.

3. The gradual development of a complex grammar in an expanding conceptual framework.

4. A mixture of hands on (enactive), illustrative (iconic), and linguistic (symbolic) experiences (cf. Bruner, 1966). As the RISD teacher describes, "the materials were presented in carefully prepared steps that used language charts as the primary diagnostic and educational tool, supplemented by films and manipulative activities such as map and graph making. The class time was divided into 30 minutes for language arts and speech and 20 minutes for project activities" (Blackwell et al., 1978, p. 128).

Baran and Aguiar (1980) developed a curriculum especially suited to the needs of late-beginning secondary-level students—most often those who are not native-born. The curriculum utilizes narratives as a means for developing language skills. A more recent approach is suggested by Simon-Olson (1982) in a set of materials prepared for hearing-impaired students. These materials utilize the concepts of the movements of peoples and the effects of cultures in contact. They are particularly well suited for the immigrant child in upper-elementary or secondary-level settings.

The commitment of these authors is to a developmental—rather than a remedial—approach to curriculum planning for the late beginner. Implicit in this perspective is the need for meaningful assessment procedures to determine where the student is in the developmental process. Teachers can then identify the next steps in the educational process and develop appropriate and effective materials for moving the student through each level.

Conclusion

We have tried to describe the various issues that must be taken into account in developing appropriate programs for hearing-impaired students from linguistically and culturally diverse backgrounds, with special reference to Hispanic populations. These issues center on the triad of child/family/school, each of which is seen as distinct but constantly interacting sociocultural entities. The implication here is that sociocultural aspects of the child and family are as important as those issues having to do specifically with the child's deafness; an appropriate educational program for the hearing-impaired child must take into account the family's and child's linguistic and cultural background. In addition, there must be a recognition that the school and its personnel reflect a particular cultural view, one which may or may not be like that of the students and families to be served. Only through understanding this cultural diversity, both in the students and ourselves, and by utilizing this diversity in a positive manner, can we develop programs that truly meet the needs of a culturally diverse population of hearing-impaired students.

References

Arredondo-Dowd, P. Personal loss and grief as a result of immigration. *Personnel and Guidance Journal*, 1981, 59 (6), 376–378.

Baran, A., & Aguiar, M. *Language and literature for the late beginner.* Providence: Corliss Park Press, 1980.

Blackwell, P., Engen, E., Fischgrund, J., & Zarcadoolas, C. *Sentences and other systems: A language and learning curriculum for hearing-impaired students.* Washington, D.C.: A. G. Bell Association for the Deaf, 1978.

Bruner, J. *Toward a theory of instruction.* Cambridge: Harvard University Press, 1966.

Bruner, J. *Beyond the information given.* New York: Norton, 1973.

Delgado, G. Hearing-impaired children from non-native language homes. *American Annals of the Deaf*, 1981, *126*, 118–121. An adaptation of this article may be found on pages 28–36.

Delgado, M., & Humm-Delgado, D. Natural support systems: Source of strength in Hispanic communities. *Social Work*, 1982, 27 (1), 83–89.

Figler, C. *Dynamics of Hispanic family systems.* Paper presented at the New York State Department of Education Invitational Conference, Albany, May 6–7, 1981.

Figler, C. LISTO presentation, Boston, April 24, 1982.

Fischgrund, J. Language intervention for hearing-impaired children from linguistically and culturally diverse backgrounds. *Topics in Language Disorders*, 1982, 2 (3), 57–66. An adaptation of this article may be found on pages 94–104.

Kubler-Ross, E. *On death and dying.* New York: Macmillan, 1969.

Lerman, A. & Cortez, E. *Discovering and meeting the needs of Hispanic hearing-impaired children* (Report, CREED VII project). New York: Lexington School for the Deaf, 1977.

Luterman, D. *Counseling parents of hearing-impaired children.* Boston: Little, Brown, 1979.

Simon-Olson, B. *People changing: The Irish come to America.* Providence: Corliss Park Press, 1982.

12

A Model for School Services to Hispanic Hearing-Impaired Children

Alan Lerman and Carmiña Vilá

At the beginning of the 1981–82 school year, the Lexington School for the Deaf initiated a coordinated bilingual/bicultural program. The process of developing the program and its staffing had begun six years earlier, in 1975, with the initiation of the CREED VII project in New York State and Projecto Oportunidad in Rhode Island.

The CREED (Cooperative Research Endeavors in the Education of the Deaf) program involved a series of projects approved by the New York State Education Department and by the consortium, New York Schools for the Deaf and Blind. The Lexington School for the Deaf began CREED VII in collaboration with St. Francis de Sales School for the Deaf (Brooklyn), St. Joseph's School for the Deaf (Bronx), JHS-47 School for the Deaf (Manhattan), and the various public Schools for Language and Hearing Impaired Children. The project examined the current status and functioning of Hispanic deaf students and their families. It experimented with methods and systems to overcome the educational disadvantages of this population.

Projecto Oportunidad, funded by the Rhode Island State Education Department, was developed and implemented at the Rhode Island School for the Deaf. Its purpose was to offer improved instructional services to Portuguese and Hispanic students.

The staff of these two separate projects—CREED VII and Projecto Oportunidad—were brought together to develop Latino In-Service Training and Orientation (LISTO), a federally funded project to train educational staff in delivery of improved services to Hispanic hearing-impaired students and their families. The ideas implemented at the Lexington School grew out of this collaboration with the Rhode Island School for the Deaf.

The Hispanic Resource Team

The first formal meeting of the Hispanic Resource Team (HRT)—the core staff for Lexington's bilingual/bicultural program—was held in September 1981. Prior to that meeting, the eight educational supervisors each developed lists of Hispanic students, their perceived needs, and the respective priorities for services to be requested from the HRT. Criteria for development of individual lists had been discussed by the supervisory group beforehand to facilitate consensus and enable each supervisor to know the concerns of colleagues. The group included the educational director, the lower-school supervisor, two part-time Hispanic resource teachers, a Hispanic social worker, a Hispanic paraprofessional, and a Spanish-language evaluator. The five Hispanic team members, all part-time, equaled one and one-half full-time positions.

Role of the Educational Director

The educational director has been of critical importance to the success of the Hispanic Resource Team. The director provides guidance for the HRT, acts as a facilitator with other units of school, offers leadership in the development of activities, and indirectly legitimizes the program to the rest of the staff. In turn, the director has an opportunity to develop understanding of the philosophy and purposes of the Hispanic program, become sensitized to the needs of Hispanic students and their families, and appreciate the complexities of delivery of these services. For example, the first decision of the group was to delay all specific instructional and social service activities until November. This was done to permit the HRT members to make personal contact with each family. The families could use this initial contact to discuss problems or to obtain information that they would not have sought directly. The educational director understood that Hispanics place a high value on personal relationships and that this cultural factor is important in home-school relations. This, he explained, justified the initial delay of services.

Role of the Educational Supervisors

The educational supervisors are important in the day-to-day functioning of the Hispanic Resource Team. They are the cement that holds all the pieces together. They are sensitive to the ongoing pressures and the atmosphere of the school, and they know the attitudes and competencies of the teachers and instructional assistants. The supervisors explain the HRT and its activities to the staff. They also help the HRT members understand the educational system and general needs of the staff. All activities are coordinated and approved by the respective educational supervisor. Staff requests for special services, emergency home visits, intake evaluations, or translators and interpreters go through the supervisor.

The educational director and the supervisors are critically important to integrating HRT activities into the regular school program. The integration of the HRT into the whole school program seems more beneficial than arranging a self-contained, separate Hispanic program. Under the existing model the student remains in the regular program while being offered additional assistance. This assistance is given by the Spanish language evaluator, the Hispanic resource teacher, and the Hispanic social worker.

The Language Evaluator

Hispanic hearing-impaired students have demonstrated lower academic performance than non-Hispanic hearing-impaired children, especially in the areas of English vocabulary and reading comprehension (Jensema, 1975; Lerman & Cortez, 1977). A disproportionate number of hearing-impaired students from non-English-speaking homes are classified as having additional handicapping conditions compared with hearing-impaired students from the general population (see chapter 3).

Currently, one-quarter of the student body at the Lexington School is from Hispanic backgrounds. During the last few years the Hispanic population at the Lexington School has more than doubled. Recognizing the serious academic problems facing many of our students, language assessment and prescription in English and Spanish are crucial. Our goals include establishing students' developmental level and proficiency in their home language and ensuring that an appropriate placement in an educational program is available to non-English-speaking hearing-impaired students.

Rationale for Assessment

Some of the academic difficulties experienced by students are related to conflicts in acquiring both home and school languages. Many

Hispanic students demonstrate some ability to function in Spanish. In the past their knowledge of the home language and culture was not considered in planning their educational program. At intake, culturally inappropriate tests were administered. Because no Spanish language tests were administered, the English language assessment appeared to indicate that these students had "no language."

Insistence by the school on English and/or sign as the languages of instruction brings with it the risk of disrupting the natural flow of communication that has been established in the home language. The home language is the deaf child's first language. "Since exposure to language is the first step in language development, hearing-impaired children entering educational programs, no matter how severe their hearing loss, have already begun the process of language acquisition" (Fischgrund, 1982, pp. 58–59).

Determination of Need for Assessment

Hispanic students who may need a thorough assessment in Spanish are referred to the evaluator by both the Pupil Personnel Office (which handles all new students) and the supervisors and classroom teachers. As part of the intake procedure all prospective Hispanic students and their families are seen by the Spanish-language evaluator, who determines whether or not a full assessment in Spanish is necessary. For example, we may see third-generation parents who are assimilated into the mainstream culture and whose Spanish language skills are extremely limited. In this case no further Spanish evaluation is necessary. Alternatively, a child recently arrived from South America who received instruction in Spanish while there will likely need a full Spanish evaluation. Most entering students can be placed somewhere between these extremes.

Students who have been enrolled in the school for some time are referred to the language evaluator by teachers who, through inservice education, begin to realize that the child's poor performance could be attributable to the discrepancy between the home and the school in terms of linguistic and sociocultural environment (individual aspirations, ethnic identification, and values). Teachers and supervisors also request services from the evaluator when they need to explore new teaching strategies that take into consideration the student's language and culture. An effective individualized education plan (IEP) should reflect knowledge of the student's background.

Special Consideration

Before any Spanish language assessment takes place, the evaluator formulates a plan of action based on the sociolinguistic background of the child. This information is critical to the assessment process. It is gathered through interviews with parents and teachers and from school reports.

Sociolinguistic background information that is helpful in planning the evaluation procedure includes (1) the age of the child; (2) the length of time the family has resided on the U.S. mainland; (3) the language environment of the home; (4) who communicates with the child (main caretaker, main communicator); (5) how family members communicate with the child (gesture, oral, sign language); (6) what language is used and by whom (Spanish, English, both); (7) whether code-switching also is used and by whom; and (8) parents' impression of the child's communication skills.

In some of the families, variations in the language used at home have been observed. In one case the grandparents spoke Spanish only, the mother was more comfortable in English, and the father constantly code-switched (alternately used both languages, switching back and forth even within sentences).

The school setting does not always provide the best environment in which to assess the child, especially when trying to establish some rapport in a language (Spanish) which he/she may relate to the domain of the home and the community. Our experience with students who had been enrolled in schools on the U.S. mainland for some time was that many of them suppressed their knowledge of Spanish within school boundaries. They had learned the school's philosophy of "English only" during school hours. In a few cases it was not until we had established a rapport through home visits that they used Spanish. For young children especially, the home provides a more comfortable and relaxed atmosphere for the the evaluation. Parents and siblings also can be involved in the procedures.

With older students the decision about where to test depends on three factors: the length of time since arriving from a Spanish-speaking country, the ability to discriminate between the two linguistic codes (home and school), and the student's feelings about his or her ethnic background. An informal session with the child, along with the child's family and school histories, will help decide whether the home or school setting would be the more reliable context in which to measure the child's functioning in Spanish.

Spanish Language Assessment

The Spanish language assessment is conducted informally. Both the developmental and proficiency levels are established by eliciting a spontaneous sample of the student's production in Spanish (through pictures, use of toys, etc.), and by providing a comprehension test. The latter helps us to assess receptive abilities in the home language. The expressive part of the test is recorded to help the evaluator transcribe and later analyze the sample. Materials used are culturally relevant; consideration is given to the differences that exist between Hispanic groups. For example, students from various countries in Central and South America are often culturally different from each other as well as from Caribbean Hispanics.

When the child appears capable of producing both Spanish and English, equivalent English language measures are also used by an evaluator dominant in English. Comparing the Spanish and English proficiency levels helps to establish the child's linguistic dominance.

Utilizing the Assessment for Program Development

All information obtained through the assessment is shared with members of the HRT. The language evaluator, the educational supervisor, and the resource teachers develop a plan that ensures the integration of home language and culture in the student's IEP. Teaching strategies and methods are also discussed. Thereafter, the language evaluator maintains contact with the resource teacher to clarify further the student's langue status. Whenever program changes are recommended by the evaluator, the HRT makes the final decision.

The Hispanic Resource Teacher

The model for the Hispanic teacher's role described here was developed through the collaboration of the CREED VII project and Projecto Oportunidad. Prior to the development of this model, two other models were explored, both involving a self-contained classroom with a monolingual English-speaking teacher. The first model included a bilingual teacher; the second model included a bilingual paraprofessional. After initial attempts to develop these two models, it was determined that they were not replicable outside of the special projects because (a) there was a lack of appropriately trained bilingual professionals, part of the larger problem of the underrepresentation of Hispanic teachers in the education system (see chapter 2); (b) the self-contained classroom did not provide the bilingual teacher with enough flexibility to meet the needs and demands of other Hispanic students and other teachers in the school; and (c) the value of adding a bilingual staff member in a self-contained classroom tended to be limited because the regular classroom teacher was not prepared to utilize the additional language skills of that person.

The model that was adopted places the bilingual (Hispanic) resource teacher outside the classroom. Under the direction of the educational supervisor, the resource teacher conducts individual or small-group remedial activities with students, meets with teachers, and has continuing contact with parents.

Instructional Activities

The bilingual resource teacher proved to be an effective model for dealing with the demands of both the school system and the families. This teacher has provided:

1. Content instruction in Spanish. This course is for students who are dominant in Spanish and have very limited skills in English.

2. English as a second language (for the same students as above).

3. Development of home-language awareness. This course includes Spanish language instruction and is designed for students from Spanish-speaking homes who, after being in the school setting for a long time, speak only English. The students deal with communication problems that arise at home.

4. Spanish as a second language. For non-Hispanics who are interested, this course uses a multicultural approach to help develop students' appreciation for and understanding of other cultures. Because a bilingual program is also a bicultural program, a cultural awareness curriculum is integrated with all language instruction. The enrichment of the Hispanic students' language is expected to help them develop positive self-concepts and attitudes toward their own culture.

The Hispanic resource teacher advises the classroom teacher on cultural issues and helps in the development of units where Hispanic culture is incorporated. The curriculum is then enriched with the introduction of other cultures.

Assistance to Families

The bilingual resource teacher needs to have enough flexibility to be able to provide support to Hispanic families. The parents are in need of an advocate to help them establish effective communication with school personnel. Through their experiences and training the Hispanic resource teachers have learned that establishing a personal and friendly relationship with a family member is an essential aspect of the communication system. This interaction enables the resource teacher to provide advice and support to the families when it is needed and, at the same time, affords the parent the opportunity to seek the Hispanic resource teacher's help when dealing with the school system. The Hispanic resource teacher participates in individualized education plan (IEP) meetings, parent conferences, and other special sessions.

Required Competencies

To be effective and efficient a Hispanic resource teacher must develop a variety of skills. The importance of each skill may vary or change depending on the school's and the student's needs. The Hispanic resource teacher must be:

1. Proficient in written and oral Spanish and knowledgeable about Hispanic culture (as well as differences between ethnic groups).

2. Skillful in developing and implementing bilingual education programs for Hispanic deaf children.

3. Able to assist classroom teachers in the application of cultural concerns to the classroom situation and in the development and implementation of multicultural curricula.

4. Capable of establishing warm and empathetic relationships with the Hispanic families.

5. Able to serve as a liaison between the school and the Hispanic home.

6. Capable of conducting appropriate language evaluations of Hispanic hearing-impaired chidren.

Special Activities

At the present time the Lexington School for the Deaf has one Hispanic resource teacher position which is shared by two teachers. Having two people has been a positive addition to the program. Their responsibilities have been shared and divided according to their experience and areas of strength.

Although the services of these teachers are available to all the departments in the school, currently their instructional efforts are concentrated in three departments. In the Infant and Preschool Center five Hispanic families and their infants are being tutored in Spanish. Several students in the Lower School are being provided with services ranging from content instruction in Spanish to English as a second language. And one group of Hispanic high school students is receiving instruction in Spanish as a second language through a multicultural approach. There are also two groups of students from non-Hispanic homes who are taking Spanish as an elective course.

Social Services to Hispanic Families

A survey on the needs of Hispanic hearing-impaired children and their families, conducted through schools for the deaf and language impaired in the New York City area (Lerman & Cortez, 1977), characterized some of the families as follows:

> Headed by Spanish speaking mothers who immigrated from rural areas of Puerto Rico in their teens, who live in a socially isolated ghetto environment, and who are mainly supported by welfare, they seem most in need of help in organizing and improving family operations such as basic child care, nutrition, housing, and traveling. They need assistance in developing some form of social relationships since they have no contact with family members or people from the community. They do not understand the nature of their hearing-impaired child's handicap and how to effectively help that child. (p. 32)

The report also concluded that, due to linguistic and cultural barriers, the families were not utilizing the existing school or community services for assistance and information.

The Lexington School believes that offering appropriate services to the family increases the child's participation in the educational program. Connection with the family through the child allows the school to offer help that can, in many instances, be more effective than other community agencies. Hispanic families require services from the school adapted for their needs.

Social Service Activities

The school's social worker and the home/school paraprofessional provide a support system for families. They offer assistance to families interested in improving the home environment for their hearing-impaired children. Whenever a request for assistance is made, the first step is a home visit. The Hispanic social worker makes an initial psychosocial assessment that is reviewed by the HRT. In a number of cases the social worker or the home/school paraprofessional will be assigned to carry out a specific set of family services.

Home-Related Services

The Hispanic social worker/paraprofessional functions as a facilitator in obtaining appropriate medical and mental health services, welfare, housing, etc. Other home-related services include interpreting, providing transportation to the school, serving as an advocate, making referrals to out-of-school agencies when appropriate, and providing counseling to help parents deal with problems of nutrition, child-rearing practices, and behavior management. At times, siblings and other members of the family may benefit from intervention. Counseling provided by the social worker is short-term and focuses on a specific problem. Long-term counseling needs are referred, after discussion by the Hispanic Resource Team, to appropriate agencies or to the Lexington Center for Mental Health Services.

School-Related Services

More often than non-Hispanics, adolescent Hispanic students are referred to counselors for problems such as truancy. In many instances the social worker is asked by the HRT to work directly with these students. He meets with them in their homes, tries to determine the problem, and develops a plan for reentry to school. Based on his relationship with a particular family, the social worker may be asked to assist in interpersonal situations affecting the child and the family. He may act as a liaison between the child, the family, and the school staff at important meetings.

The Process of Developing Hispanic Services

The development of new services depends on a clear understanding of the needs of the group designated to receive these services.

Although the staff is informed about a number of exceptional or "problem" cases, they are not aware of the needs of the majority of Hispanic students. To become aware of the needs of these students, some practical steps should be taken. A student list should be compiled that includes information about country of origin, family situation, current academic functioning, social behavior, and parents' home language. Teachers, supervisors, and families can be contacted to obtain this information. To obtain information from families, the initial contact should be made through a native speaker of Spanish. The list should indicate the kind of services the Hispanic student has needed in the past and an evaluation of the services received.

The survey, covering every student with a Hispanic surname, both sensitizes the staff to the school's concern for improving services and gathers data that can be used in the establishment of priorities for future service. At a later date this information can be contrasted with data from subsequent surveys to determine the success of any new service or program.

For long-range planning, knowledge about the population residing in the locality is helpful. Information about population changes in the community the school serves may lead to modification in special services. It is necessary to know which Hispanic populations reside in the area because major cultural and class differences exist between and among Hispanic groups. These differences often relate to country of origin. Hispanics for whom emigration/immigration was more restricted tend to be better educated, more middle class in orientation, and more likely to have intact families. Those Hispanics who, for political or economic reasons, emigrated/immigrated more easily tend to have rural backgrounds and/or lower economic circumstances in addition to less education and fewer work skills.

Establishing Priorities

Most schools that we have contacted in our training and research activities indicate that their primary concerns are for services to adolescents and pre-adolescents. Truancy, fights, pregnancy, and poor academic functioning are listed as major problems. Another major concern is for translators and interpreters to contact families. Contact by

Hispanic staff is often required for emergencies or for parent conferences. These two elements become short-term priorities. To help prevent some of the major problems, however, there must be a long-term program that includes services to help the students academically and socially.

Resources for New Programs

We have considered three ways to staff new programs that serve Hispanic students and their families. They are: changing existing roles, hiring Hispanic staff for regular positions, and creating new positions.

1. Changing existing roles. Some staff members currently in teaching, paraprofessional, or supportive roles have additional relevant abilities. They may be Hispanic, familiar with the Spanish language, or knowledgeable about the cultural and economic background of the Spanish community. These staff members can be asked to assist in offering Hispanic services. Their responsibilities can be modified so they can have time to offer the needed services. For example, a teacher of a self-contained class who knows Spanish can be assigned a number of students from Spanish-speaking families and be given coverage to teach a Spanish language class. A Spanish-speaking instructional aide can be given release time from classroom activities to make phone contacts and do important translations for teachers in the department.

2. Hiring Hispanic staff. There are few certified Hispanic teachers of the deaf. They make significant contributions to the programs that hire them. When no certified Hispanic teacher is available, a Hispanic paraprofessional can be hired and offered assistance in educational and career development. A number of schools now have such individuals on staff. This is a long-term commitment; five years may be required for such a person to become a certified teacher of the deaf.

3. Creating new positions. The creation of new positions requires either new funding or some changes in funding patterns. Our experience indicates that funding agencies are interested and will cooperate in the attempt to develop services that meet the needs of Hispanic hearing-impaired students.

If all three of these staffing options are implemented, the actual additional cost for new services is minimal.

The Future

The development of an effective program of services within the school system has been a long process. Its roots go back to 1975 with the CREED VII project and Projecto Oportunidad. Thus far, we have seen significant improvement in the functioning of our Hispanic students. The input and support from supervisors and teachers have been critical to this success.

The program of services to Hispanic hearing-impaired students and their families is still in the process of development. As problems arise, or as we become more aware of needs that have been overlooked, new activities will be developed. But the basic direction of the program is established, and some needs are clear. Among the more important needs are the hiring of new bilingual personnel and the development of a core group of Hispanic parents.

References

Delgado, G.L. Hearing-impaired children from non-native language homes. *American Annals of the Deaf*, 1981, *126*,118–121. An adaptation of this article may be found on pages 28–36.

Fischgrund, J.E. Language intervention for hearing impaired children from linguistically and culturally diverse backgrounds. *Topics in Language Disorders*, 1982, 2(3), 57–66. An adaptation of this article may be found on pages 94–104.

Jensema, C. *The relationship between academic achievement and the demographic characteristics of hearing-impaired youth.* Washington, D.C.: Gallaudet College Office of Demographic Studies, 1975.

Lerman, A.,& Cortez, E. *Discovering and meeting the needs of Hispanic hearing-impaired children* (Report, CREED VII project). New York: Lexington School for the Deaf, 1977.

Maestas, J. *The participation of Hispanics in special education.* Paper presented at the Institute for Educational Leadership, George Washington University, Washington, D.C., March 4, 1981.

Teacher Preparation

13

Teachers of Hispanic Hearing-Impaired Children: Competencies and Preparation

June Grant

Hispanic hearing-impaired children present unique educational problems. Their poor academic achievement records attest to that fact (Lerman, 1980). For these problems to be resolved, special programs must be designed which identify and address the problems. Special programs entail special competencies for techers. This chapter examines those special competencies and explores possible delivery systems.

Background

The most detrimental aspect of hearing impairment is its concomitant obstacle to language acquisition (Kretschmer & Kretschmer, 1978). Likewise, the overriding difficulty encountered in school settings by children from Spanish-speaking homes is their inability to function comfortably, or at all, in English (Andersson & Boyer, 1960.) Not only the school language but also the Anglo, middle class culture are foreign to these children. The situation faced by Hispanic hearing-impaired children is truly unique: the acquisition of any language is a formidable task for them; and the language to which they are exposed during most of their waking hours is different from the language of the school.

The hardship is more than a combination of these two factors; it is a compounded complication with no easy solutions. Added to the duplicate language difficulties is a third factor common to many Hispanic children: poverty, a culture in itself (DeBlassie, 1976). Each of these conditions requires special knowledge and skills of personnel who aspire to lead these children to successful academic achievement. In addition to great dedication, teachers of Hispanic hearing-impaired children must have many competencies in all three areas.

It is essential for the teachers of hearing-impaired children to acquire the competencies requisite for all teachers. The National Council for Accreditation of Teacher Education (NCATE) requires that teacher preparation programs meet six standards in order to be approved. Within the standard concerning the design of curricula are two subcomponents, one dealing with multicultural education and the other with special education (NCATE, 1979). The profession recognizes the fact that all teachers must be capable of meeting some of the special needs of children.

Teachers of hearing-impaired children must have knowledge of the content, materials, and methods that comprise the curricula in programs for nonhandicapped children. The Council on Education of the Deaf (CED) requires that teachers have prerequisite knowledge in such basic areas of study as child growth and development, learning theory, general psychology, instructional procedures in general education, and the function of social institutions, among other general areas of study (CED, 1972). There are five additional standards, dealing with competencies relevant only to teaching hearing-impaired children, that CED lists as minimal in its requirements for certification. However, there is no mention of the need for competencies that sensitize teachers to the values, languages, and attitudes of minority cultures.

The lack of such a requirement is surprising given that there are areas in the United States where the "minority" cultures are the majority. For example, in the Brownsville (Texas) Regional Day School for the Deaf, more than 98 percent of the students have Spanish surnames (Office of Demographic Studies, 1981). Based on certification requirements alone, it is possible for education graduates to begin teaching at such schools having had little or no exposure to cultural pluralism.

Another serious consideration in the education of hearing-impaired children is the desperate need for early identification and parent involvement (Simmons-Martin, 1978). The advantage of early intervention for all handicapped children is well documented in the literature (Bricker & Bricker, 1976; Hayden & Haring, 1976; Horton, 1976; Painter, 1971; Shearer & Shearer, 1976). Texas, as well as other states, recognizes the importance of this early intervention and provides services for hearing-impaired children from birth to age 22 (Texas Education Agency, 1978). However, there are no specific certification standards for the personnel who provide services for infants and their parents, nor requirements which accommodate the special needs of non-English-speaking families.

The socioeconomic status of many, and in some instances most, of the hearing-impaired children from Spanish-speaking homes is another factor that requires a special competency on the part of the teachers. Almost 50 percent of the students enrolled at the Regional Day School for the Deaf in San Antonio qualify for free or reduced price lunches. To qualify for these benefits, family income must be below a specified level. Since poverty is a culture with its own sanctions and prohibitions (DeBlassie, 1976), teachers need to become sensitive to the parameters of poverty and to acquire competencies that will enable them to gain the confidence of that population. Thus, it would seem that the profession is in need of teachers of hearing-impaired children who have competencies as teachers, as teachers of hearing-impaired children, as teachers of children from various non-English-speaking backgrounds, as teacher/counselors of hearing-impaired infants and their parents, and as teachers of children who are economically deprived.

To prepare teachers who are thoroughly competent in all these areas would be an overwhelming task requiring more coursework and practicum experience than most preparation programs can provide. For example, some geographic areas do not have high concentrations of ethnic minorities with whom the students can gain experience. Yet, if programs are to meet NCATE standards, students will have at least theoretical if not practical knowledge of different cultural settings. An analogous situation might exist concerning parent/infant intervention competencies. If early-infant services are not mandated by legislation and no parent/infant programs exist in the geographic area, preparation programs cannot offer practicum activities in their curricula. The number of economically deprived hearing-impaired children may likewise be minimal. However, teachers in preparation do not necessarily teach in the setting in which they prepared. Therefore, programs for hearing-impaired children may have to provide inservice staff development in order for their teachers to meet the distinct needs of their populations.

Three Components

The three components of a teacher's background and preparation that may be lacking and that may directly affect Hispanic hearing-impaired children, then, are knowledge and skills in teaching children from Spanish-speaking homes, children from economically depressed homes, and infants and their parents. There is a great deal of obvious overlap among these components, as in the case of a hearing-impaired infant whose parents speak only Spanish and whose family income is at the poverty level. This hypothetical situation is not farfetched, particularly in the states with large Spanish-speaking populations such as Texas, California, Arizona, and New York. Therefore, discussion of the three areas will also necessarily overlap.

The literature now reveals some research and concern for the preparation of teachers of handicapped children from nondominant language and cultural settings (Bergin, 1980; Grant, 1972; Prieto et al., 1981; Pynn, 1980). Much of the knowledge gleaned has its foundation in pioneering work in bilingual/bicultural education. The National Association for Bilingual Education publishes its journal three times a year, and the National Clearinghouse for Bilingual Education can provide a computer search using any of five databases. The general movement in favor of bilingual education has generated a plethora of literature to guide special educators in the execution of their programs. The curricula should be influenced by current research which shows that children acquire a second language in ways very similar to native language acquisition (Lindfors, 1980); that the best medium for children's learning, especially during their young years, is their native language (Andersson & Boyer, 1970); that good readers in a first language transfer this skill into their second language (Goodman, Goodman, & Flores, 1980); and that the ability to know two symbols for one object or action promotes metalinguistic awareness (Cazden, 1972), which goes beyond linguistic competence and is perhaps related to language learning and cognitive development (Bewell & Straw, 1981).

These findings, among many others, are valuable, and such research certainly should be included in the preservice curricula. However, the research is not completely applicable to hearing-impaired children because, in many cases, these children have few if any first or native language skills or language acquisition strategies. Yet hearing-impaired children possess a predisposition to acquire language (Lenneberg, 1964). Therefore, any strategies to promote fluency in two languages for hearing-impaired children should be modifiable to accommodate the language deficit of these children (Furth, 1973).

The literature also contains valuable information concerning various language learning styles, types of experiences, and values of children from economically deprived environments (Hass, 1971; Moore, 1971; Sigel, 1971). These important findings also need to be included in the curricula of preparation programs. In addition, the benefits gained from infant intervention programs for hearing-impaired children are most encouraging, and CED certification standards require that students develop skills in counseling parents who are, in reality, the teachers of infants (CED, 1972).

In summary, teachers of Hispanic hearing-impaired children need knowledge and skills in addition to those acquired in most preparation programs if they are to deal competently with the additional handicaps that this population often presents.

Special Competencies

Though the literature concerning the preparation of teachers for Hispanic handicapped children is sparse, one can infer clusters of competencies considered essential (Bergin, 1980; Grant, 1972; Prieto et al., 1981; Pynn, 1980). The need for teachers to be able to counsel parents and involve them in their children's education is viewed as an essential component in all programs. Another high priority is in-depth knowledge of the minority culture and language. These two components appear to share equal importance with more instructional competencies such as knowledge of linguistics: language acquisition and assessment, language disorders, bilingualism, linguistic theory. Other competencies, such as instructional strategies; evaluation systems; and knowledge of research, legislation, and community resources, are likewise essential and must be included in the curricula.

An examination of the first three competencies—the ability to involve parents, knowledge of the language and culture, and knowledge of linguistics—is fundamental in discussing the preparation of teachers for Hispanic hearing-impaired children. The importance of the parental role in education of Hispanic hearing-impaired children cannot be overemphasized, nor can the fact that the parents of these children can improve their parenting skills and their children's development through the assistance of professional guidance and counseling. Schaeffer-Dresler (1981) has shown that limited English-speaking parents improved their language stimulating skills and ability to attend to their children's communicative intents through instruction and use of their native language. Preservice or inservice teachers must develop the ability to involve parents in the educational process.

The most desirable teacher/counselor will serve the family in its dominant language; this can be a problem, however, due to the dearth of Spanish-speaking professionals (Lerman, 1980). Preparation programs should endeavor to recruit minority students if this problem is to be ameliorated (Prieto et al., 1981). It is difficult, if not impossible, to support parents who are not fluent in English—and neither knowledgeable about nor comfortable with Anglo culture—by communicating through an interpreter or in English. The educational and cultural barriers between the parents and the professional can be strong: The parents are easily intimidated by the medical and educational vocabulary; they have little self-confidence and low self-esteem; and they do not want to discuss private matters with strangers (Wilson-Portuondo, 1980).

Preparation programs can help resolve these problems by cultivating cultural and social sensitivities. For example, teachers need to be able to help parents understand the U.S. educational system, which may be very different from the one in their native land; they need to be able to assist parents in enhancing their self-concepts; and they need to be able to identify and utilize the natural, available support systems such as strong family ties, friends, and community spirit (Wilson-Portuondo, 1980).

In addition to services that directly support the parents, there is another cluster of competencies for teachers to acquire for interaction with parents—competencies which more directly affect the development and academic achievement of the children. For example, teachers must be able to help parents define realistic goals for their hearing-impaired children, help parents with behavior management, demonstrate language stimulation techniques, explain the function and use of auditory amplification, and optimize the development of creativity. These few obvious competencies are imperative if programs are to achieve any degree of success.

The second competency, knowledge of the language and culture, presents a different set of parameters. Ideally, teachers/counselors would be native speakers of the language and members of the culture, but this is seldom the case, especially the latter. Hispanic professionals are few; more often than not they are from middle class backgrounds and share many Anglo cultural values. However, membership in the culture does not guarantee successful teaching (Rueda et al., 1981), and all teachers should be sensitized to the integrity of minority cultural values (NCATE, 1979). The essential competencies in this cluster require knowledge of biculturalism: how it affects learning; how the two cultures conflict in religion, family size and relationships, value judgments, child rearing practices, health practices, and life styles; and how to help the child assimilate the dominant culture without displacing his/her home culture (Grant, 1972).

The third competency, knowledge of linguistics, is of vital importance in all preparation programs. The CED standards require that at least three-tenths of a program be devoted to acquiring knowledge and skill in developing language and communication for hearing-impaired children (CED, 1972). Teachers must have knowledge of the language acquisition process for all children, the implictions of linguistic theory, the administration and interpretation of language assessment and evaluation instruments, the research and literature in the discipline, and the language programs that are effective with hearing-impaired children (Bergin, 1980; Grant, 1972; Pynn, 1980; Rueda et al., 1981).

In addition to these competencies, teachers of Hispanic hearing-impaired children must have skills which enable them to determine whether children's language learning difficulties are due to second language acquisition, hearing impairment, or language disability. There is also the big question: In what language should instruction take place—English? Spanish? American Sign Language (ASL)? Resolution of this dilemma is beyond the scope of this paper, but teachers and administrators must give serious consideration to this question. If abundant language stimulation for the child is to be offered in the home, more than likely the language of instruction will have to be the language with which the parents are more comfortable. Schaeffer-Dresler (1981) found that when one family in her study decided to introduce English as the language of the home, instead of the dominant Spanish, they experienced difficulty; the amount of verbal stimulation was decreased, objects were labeled with single words, and there were frequent occurrences of incorrect grammar. The problem of which language, or two languages, or three languages (including ASL) probably is best resolved on an individual basis (Lerman, 1980). Further research and longitudinal studies must be done before any generalizations can be made.

The three clusters of competencies detailed are not the only ones teachers of Hispanic hearing-impaired children need in order to enable effective learning in their students. There are other important competencies that comprise the special curriculum. Some of these are: knowledge of instructional strategies and materials for bilingual learners, ability to sensitize administrative officers and colleagues to the instructional and resource needs of Hispanic hearing-impaired children, knowledge of legislation affecting the education of handicapped and linguistically different pupils, and knowledge of current research in bilingual/bicultural education. These competencies are requisite in addition to the general ones. The question of how and in what setting these competencies are achieved is another matter.

Preparation Program Models

It seems apparent that teachers of Hispanic hearing-impaired children need competencies and skills over and beyond those acquired in traditional programs. The important issue is how to provide the opportunity to obtain the necessary knowledge and skills. Traditional preservice programs, both graduate and undergraduate, have little time for extra coursework and practicum experiences if they meet NCATE and CED standards. The *American Annals of the Deaf* 1982 directory of programs and services for the deaf lists programs that prepare professional specialists in areas such as rehabilitation, parent/infant training, leadership training, and counseling. Most of the programs listed are graduate level, implying undergraduate backgrounds in the education of hearing-impaired children. A special program to prepare teachers in bilingual education for Hispanic hearing-impaired children would be one model. Such a program would need to be located in a geographic area that could ensure abundant practicum experiences with the target population.

Another possible model is a preservice program coordinating the existing programs in a university. For example, a university that offers one program in bilingual education and another in education of the hearing impaired could combine its resources. One possibility is to infuse the additional material into existing courses rather than to create new courses that would extend the required preparation time. Blanco (1977) states that the only solution to the lack of university personnel with pedagogical backgrounds as well as fluency in two languages is genuine cooperation among the various disciplines. Teachers of bilingual children and teachers of handicapped children need to be aware of each other's disciplines, because many children are members of both groups (Abbott, 1975).

The arguments for preservice programs can be countered with those in favor of inservice models. Several successful inservice models are described in this book and in the larger literature. The CREED (Cooperative Research Endeavors in Education of the Deaf) project in New York City devised six delivery models of service and determined that two were particularly effective—the resource teacher model and the home/school paraprofessional model (see chapter 12; see also Lerman, 1980). In the former model certain teachers were selected to receive special training and become resource teachers for teachers with Hispanic hearing-impaired children in their classes. The resource teachers have proved especially helpful in the intake and assessment procedures, in instructing children in Spanish or English as a second language (ESL), and in assisting with family matters that affect the children's classroom functioning. The home/school paraprofessional program has been an important factor in helping parents to prepare their children for the educational process (Lerman & Cortez, 1978).

The LISTO (Latino In-Service Training and Orientation) project utilizes the resource teacher model, which is a compromise between the children's instructional needs and the lack of appropriately trained bilingual professionals. The salient feature of the LISTO project is that the resource teacher works as a liaison with other staff within the school and with the support of the administration (Lerman, 1980). A similar project, Projecto Oportunidad, exists at the Rhode Island School for the Deaf and serves a group of Portuguese-speaking families from the Azores that has settled in the area (see chapter 11; see also Lerman, 1980).

Another alternative for enabling teachers to provide appropriate services to Hispanic handicapped children is a networking system (Pynn, 1980). This model involves not only teacher education but also comprehensive cooperation and awareness of available personnel resources—instructional, administrative, and community. Still another model is a teacher corps model developed jointly by the Edgewood Independent School District and Trinity University in San Antonio, Texas (Utley & Leslie, 1982). This model was developed as an alternative to the traditional inservice education for bilingual teachers. Instructional support teachers—teachers with teaching experience but no current teaching responsibilities—serve solely as support personnel to other teachers. This model was designed for nonhandicapped Hispanic students, but such a model could be adapted easily to teachers of hearing-impaired children. Other models exist, some specifically designed for hearing-impaired students and others initially designed for nonhandicapped students, that can be effective in teaching Hispanic hearing-impaired children. Personnel in programs with unique circumstances should be encouraged to design models that will satisfy their needs.

The Challenge

Hispanic hearing-impaired children continue to encounter more difficulties in acquiring language than do hearing-impaired children from the dominant culture. The problems faced by these children must be resolved; if they are not, the profession is failing a large segment of the population. Hispanic hearing-impaired children have the potential to acquire useful language, maybe even two languages. The profession must find suitable means by which the children can realize that potential and achieve academic success.

References

Abbott, E. *Learning disabilities—they're all around you.* Paper presented at the International Bilingual Bicultural Education Conference, Chicago, May 1975. (ERIC Document Reproduction Service No. ED 128 529)

American Annals of the Deaf, 1982, *127* (2).

Andersson, T., & Boyer, M. *Bilingual schooling in the United States* (Vol. 1). Washington, D.C.: Government Printing Office, 1970.

Bergin, V. *Special education needs in bilingual programs.* Washington, D.C.: National Clearinghouse for Bilingual Education, 1980. (ERIC Document Reproduction Service No. ED 197 527)

Bewell, D.V., & Straw, S.B. Metalinguistic awareness, cognitive development and language learning. In Froese & Straw, *Research in the language arts.* Baltimore: University Park Press, 1981.

Blanco, G. The education perspective. In *Bilingual education: Current perspectives.* Arlington, Va.: Center for Applied Linguistics, 1977. (ERIC Document Reproduction Service No. ED 146 822)

Bricker, W.A., & Bricker, D.D. The infant, toddler, and preschool research and intervention project. In T.D. Tjossem (Ed.), *Intervention strategies for high risk infants and young children.* Baltimore: University Park Press, 1976.

Cazden, C.B. *Child language and education.* New York: Holt, Rinehart and Winston, 1972.

Council on Education of the Deaf. *Standards for the certification of teachers of the hearing-impaired.* Silver Spring, Md.: Author, 1972.

DeBlassie, R.R. *Counseling with Mexican American youth: Preconceptions and processes.* Austin, Tex.: Learning Concepts, 1976.

Furth, H.G. *Deafness and learning.* Belmont, Calif.: Wadsworth, 1973.

Goodman, K., Goodman, Y., & Flores, B. *Reading in the bilingual classroom: Literacy and biliteracy.* Washington, D.C.: National Clearinghouse for Bilingual Education, National Institute of Education, 1979. (ERIC Reproduction Service No. ED 181 725)

Grant, J. *Proceedings of a workshop on the preparation of personnel in education of bilingual hearing-impaired children, ages 0–4.* San Antonio: Trinity University, 1972.

Hass, W.A. On the heterogeneity of psychological processes in syntactic development. In C.S. Lavatelli (Ed.), *Language training in early childhood education.* Urbana: University of Illinois Press for ERIC Clearinghouse on Early Childhood Education, 1971.

Hayden, A., & Haring, N.G. Early intervention for high risk infants and young children: Programs for Down's Syndrome children. In T.D. Tjossem (Ed.), *Intervention strategies for high risk infants and young children.* Baltimore: University Park Press, 1976.

Horton, K.B. Early intervention for hearing-impaired infants and young children. In T.D. Tjossem (Ed.), *Intervention strategies for high risk infants and young children.* Baltimore: University Park Press, 1976.

Kretschmer, R.R., & Kretschmer, L.W. *Development and intervention with the hearing impaired.* Baltimore: University Park Press, 1978.

Lenneberg, E. A biological perspective of language. In E. Lenneberg, (Ed.), *New directions in the study of language.* Cambridge: M.I.T. Press, 1964.

Lerman, A. Improving service to Hispanic hearing-impaired students: Relationship to bilingual education. In *Proceedings of a workshop on special education personnel preparation* (Center of Adult Education, University of Maryland, February 1980). Washington, D.C.: Association for Cross Cultural Education and Social Studies, 1980. (ERIC Document Reproduction Service No. ED 189 795)

Lerman, A.,& Cortez, E. *Discovering and meeting the needs of Hispanic hearing-impaired children.* Albany: New York State Education Department, 1978. (ERIC Document Reproduction Service No. ED 155 292)

Lindfors, J. *Children's language and learning.* Englewood Cliffs, N.J.: Prentice-Hall, 1980.

Moore, D.R. Language research and preschool language training. In C.S. Lavatelli (Ed.), *Language training in early childhood education.* Urbana: University of Illinois Press for ERIC Clearinghouse on Early Childhood Education, 1971.

National Council for Accreditation of Teacher Education. *Standards for the accreditation of teacher education.* Washington, D.C.: Author, 1979.

Office of Demographic Studies, Gallaudet College. *Reporting source summary: Texas survey of hearing-impaired children and youth, 1980–81.* Washington, D.C.: Author, 1981.

Pointer, G. A tutorial language program for disadvantaged infants. In C.S. Lavatelli (Ed.), *Language training in early childhood education.* Urbana: University of Illinois Press for ERIC Cleringhouse on Early Childhood Education, 1971.

Prieto, A.G., Rueda, R.S., & Rodriguez, R.F. Teaching competencies for bilingual/multicultural exceptional children.*Teacher Education and Special Education,* 1981,4(4), 35–39.

Pynn, M.E. Issues in bilingual/bicultural special education personnel preparation. In *Proceedings of a workshop on special education personnel preparation* (Center of Adult Education, University of Maryland, February 1980). Washington, D.C.: Association for Cross Cultural Education and Social Studies, 1980. (ERIC Document Reproduction Service No. ED 189 795)

Rueda, R.S., Rodriguez, R.F. & Prieto, A.G. Teachers' perceptions of competencies for instructing bilingual/multicultural exceptional children. *Exceptional Children,* 1981, 48(3), 268–270.

Schaeffer-Dresler. *Hearing-impaired children from Spanish-speaking homes.* Unpublished master's thesis, California State University, Los Angeles, 1981.

Shearer, D.E., & Shearer, M.S. The portage project: A model for early childhood intervention. In T.D. Tjossem (Ed.), *Intervention strategies for high risk infants and young children.* Baltimore: University Park Press, 1976.

Sigel, I. Language of the disadvantaged: The distancing hypothesis. In C.S. Lavatelli (Ed.), *Language training in early childhood education.* Urbana: University of Illinois Press for ERIC Clearinghouse on Early Childhood Education, 1971.

Simmons-Martin, A.A. Early management procedure for the hearing-impaired child. In F.N. Martin (Ed.), *Pediatric audiology.* Englewood Cliffs, N.J.: Prentice-Hall, 1978.

Texas Education Agency. *Policies and administrative procedures for the education of handicapped students.* Austin: Author, 1978.

Utley, C., & Leslie, J. *Teacher corps model programs.* Unpublished report, Edgewood Independent School District and Trinity University, San Antonio, Tex., 1982.

Wilson-Portuondo, M. Parent-school communication: A two-way approach. In *Proceedings of a workshop on special education personnel preparation* (Center of Adult Education, University of Maryland, February 1980). Washington, D.C.: Association for Cross Cultural Education and Social Studies, 1980. (ERIC Document Reproduction Service No. ED 189 795)

14

Outreach Programs for the Hispanic Deaf: One Model

Harriet Green Kopp

In 1970 the Department of Communicative Disorders at San Diego State University (SDSU) established a preparation program for educators of the deaf under the direction of this professor. As part of the outreach program for the Hispanic hearing impaired, a private day school for the deaf, La Escuela Orales Auditivos, was supported in Tijuana. It was staffed with a qualified bilinguial principal, Janet Thompson, who was a graduate student in the program. The university provided audiological testing, clinical assessment of pupils, medical referrals, curricular materials, and hearing aids. Inservice training, including demonstration teaching, was made available for teachers recruited as graduates of the teacher's colleges of Baja California and Mexico City. San Diego State University faculty and graduate students from the Department of Communicative Disorders spent one day a week at the school. Mexican students came to the campus for diagnostic assessment and clinical intervention. As the first and only school for the deaf in Tijuana, it served as a unique site for preparing SDSU faculty and student audiologists and teachers of the deaf to assess and to teach Hispanic pupils who had no prior access to language learning or education. Despite the school's title, transmission modes were eclectic because many pupils were 12 years or older on admission and had no prior education. A series of articulation, phonologic, and language test batteries designed for Hispanic speakers was developed and field tested as graduate student projects. Students also field tested instruments developed at other universities. In 1975, when the school had an enrollment of more than 125 pupils, it was taken over by the minister of education of Baja California. Unfortunately, it is no longer operative.

This chapter and chapter 6 are expansions of a paper prepared for the International Congress on Education of the Deaf, Hamburg, West Germany, August 4–8, 1980 (Kopp, 1982, pp. 186–188).

By 1972, two Hispanic outreach health clinics had been established on the U. S. side of the border, in San Ysidro and San Diego. The speech, hearing, and language units of these clinics were served by faculty audiologists, speech pathologists, and graduate students supplied by the SDSU Department of Communicative Disorders. As the clinics grew, they assumed financial responsibility for staffing (with university approval of personnel), and they continue to serve as practicum sites. Severely hearing-impaired individuals of all ages are referred for clinical assessment and intervention to the university on-campus communication clinics and to the appropriate school districts.

Teacher Preparation

There are three sizable school centers for Hispanic hearing-impaired children in Chula Vista, San Diego City, and Carlsbad. Each employs bilingual teachers (at least one in each center with fluent Spanish) and a number of Hispanic bilingual teaching assistants. These programs have a close, cooperative relationship with the SDSU teacher preparation program for the deaf, providing exciting practicum and research experiences for students. They also assist the Department of Communicative Disorders in its search for high quality Hispanic recruits, and they become employers of the bi/trilingual graduates.

Bilingual School Programs

Bilingual school programs for the hearing have been well supported by state and federal grants. Programs for the bilingual deaf have not grown as rapidly despite a demonstrated need. The lack of programs for the deaf across the Mexican border has encouraged both transient and permanent in-migration. A number of small bilingual programs have been developed in the past decade throughout California, centered mostly in large cities and associated with university teacher preparation programs. To date, these programs have not developed a central, organized thrust. Rather, they appear to be in initial, exploratory growth stages of identifying population needs and developing curricula and methods.

A prime local concern has been in the area of the early identification of young hearing-impaired children and the encouragement of Hispanic families to enroll their youngsters in the schools. Their reluctance appears to arise from prior experience with the limitations of general public education in Mexico and Central America and from the tendency in

Mexican-Hispanic culture to shelter the handicapped within the family and to rely on the family network rather than public agencies for support. In many instances, the low socioeconomic levels of in-migrants, their alien status, and their dysfluency in English add to their avoidance of either medical or educational consultation. When children are identified, they have had little exposure to a communication system or to conceptual language beyond a familial gesture code. School placement is difficult; a preteenage child of normal nonverbal intelligence with no functional communication ability, language structure, or content is prepared neither for special nor mainstream education for the hearing impaired. It is estimated that almost one-quarter of the hearing-impaired children in the San Diego city and county school districts come from families where the primary language spoken is Spanish. Their children vary widely in range of communication ability, educational experience, and language competencies.

Trilingual Education

Because the Hispanic families with hearing-impaired children are scattered within two large counties, San Diego and Imperial, counseling parents has been a continuing problem. A recent experimental approach has involved the development of videotaped programs—the *Trilingual Education Series* (Christensen, 1982)—designed chiefly to provide instruction in conceptual sign for Spanish-speaking families. The series is accompanied by an illustrated manual including direct translations in English and Spanish of video scripts and additional exercises for classroom and home practice. Signs included are those used in local and regional schools. Where there are variations, the variations are explained as each sign is presented with both English and Spanish spoken interpretation. Concepts are presented first in English with the accompanying sign and then in Spanish with the sign repeated. A serendipity reported by some Spanish monolingual parents is that they are learning English as well as sign language. The program also has been used to instruct English speakers in Spanish. The signs and language concepts have been selected to be of practical value in the home. The series has been broadcast on the local Public Broadcasting Service channel and also is available to Spanish-speaking families at various centrally located Instructional Television Fixed Service (ITFS) receivers.

While only a few families may become truly trilingual (Spanish, English, sign), it is hoped that sign will establish a conceptual base language and useful transmission mode, especially for deaf children with essentially Spanish monolingual families. At the same time, opportunity is provided for families to receive systematic exposure to English, sign, and the conceptual language required for preschool readiness. In the initial stage, only a small number of families have continued participation. Expansion of the pilot program to a larger population is planned.

Portable VTR equipment also has been used to tape Hispanic students in the classroom and clinic. These tapes are viewed in the home and discussed by the family and a trilingual graduate student clinician from the deaf education program. Videotapes also may be recorded in the home and viewed by teacher, support staff, clinicians, and others. This permits a nonthreatening initiation to interaction between home and school. Additional videotapes, designed for teachers in training, have been made of discussions between parents and professionals; they illuminate the issues, problems, and cultural values relevant to the rights and concerns of children and families from non-English-speaking, Hispanic settings.

Clinic and Fieldwork Practica

The Department of Communicative Disorders also provides on-campus clinical sessions with individual tutoring in speech and language. The transmission modes available are eclectic. Those used are selected after consultation with parents, school, diagnostician, and child on the basis of initial and ongoing assessments. The clinicians for Hispanic children are graduate students majoring in deaf education. They are either bilingual or trained in Spanish and are prepared to use all transmission modes. They are supervised closely by qualified faculty. An interdisciplinary course is available for those undergraduate and graduate majors in communicative disorders who desire to develop fluency in Spanish and sign language. The course is cotaught by faculty from the Departments of Spanish and Communicative Disorders.

To further advance their level of competency, the graduate students have fieldwork placements in classrooms for the hearing impaired. The fieldworkers must be fluent in English, Spanish, and sign. Their assignments include daily direct tutoring of individual Hispanic children; translation of messages to parents; home visitation with parents; and, as necessary, a liaison role between school and home. University faculty and school teachers share in the planning and supervision of each individualized program.

Another experimental approach is the Extended Day Program operated jointly by the Chula Vista School District and SDSU Department of Communicative Disorders. Fieldwork students from the university provide after-school enrichment activities for Hispanic deaf children. The high interest, language-based projects are developed and implemented under the joint supervision of a creative trilingual teacher of the deaf from the Chula Vista schools and a university faculty member. Children are transported by the district.

The concept of fieldwork in classes for the deaf by all undergraduate and graduate majors in deaf education, under close joint supervision of a classroom teacher and a university faculty member, was developed in 1971 as an experiential prelude to individual and small group clinical experiences. Several semesters of clinical practicum under direct supervision of university faculty and a semester of practicum in a classroom for hearing children precede the practicum experience in a class for the deaf. For selected students who have attained the requisite academic, clinical, and trilingual competency, additional experiences with Hispanic children are available. Many of these students had high competency in sign or were fluent in Spanish prior to admission to the program. Students majoring in audiology, speech pathology, or child language are encouraged to join the deaf education majors in the trilingual preparation courses. In all of the practicum, didactic, and special skill courses, students are exposed to the cultural values and special concerns of the Hispanic community.

Evaluation

The organizational framework for joint bilingual service programs has been developed, implemented, and operated cooperatively by the SDSU Department of Communicative Disorders, the school districts, and a number of public and private agencies during the past decade. The more recent development and implementation of the trilingual programs, however, should be credited to Professors Kathee Christensen (Communicative Disorders) and Ben Christensen (Spanish Department).* As each of the programs has matured, preliminary evaluation of the

*In developing program materials to serve the Hispanic hearing impaired, the Department of Communicative Disorders has had the ongoing support of SDSU's College of Human Services, the Spanish Department, and the Department of Multicultural Education.

effectiveness of intervention strategies, materials, and personnel preparation has been instituted. In general, community advisory groups, including consumers, have assisted in the assessment of each of the projects and in ongoing modification of goals and objectives. The major goal of improving access to education for the Hispanic deaf has challenged the faculty and community to explore innovative paths, some of which may be appropriate for adaptation by other communities.

References

Christensen, K. Utilization of videotape programs as educational enrichment for Spanish-speaking families and their deaf children. *American Annals of the Deaf,* 1980, *125*(6), 841–843.

Christensen, K. *Trilingual education series.* San Diego: San Diego State University Learning Resource Center Foundation, 1982.

Kopp, H. Bilingual Problems: Mexican-Americans, American-Indians. In *Proceedings of the International Congress on Education of the Deaf,* Hamburg, West Germany, August 4–8, 1980 (Vol. 2). Heidelberg: J. Groos Verlag, 1982.

Resources

Because interest in the Hispanic hearing-impaired population is relatively new, specific resources are not in great abundance. Teachers, parents, students, and other professionals might want to contact contributors to this volume (see pages iii–iv) for further information on particular concerns. For example, June Grant, Harriet Kopp, and Alan Lerman are involved in teacher training programs related to bilingual hearing-impaired students. (Another good contact on teacher training is Maria Brisk, Ph.D., Bilingual Education Program, Boston University, 605 Commonwealth Avenue, Boston, MA 02215.)

Many projects designed to meet the needs of bilingual handicapped children are in operation. A fairly complete description of these can be found in *Bridging the Gap between Bilingual and Special Education*, by P. Landurand (Reston, Va.: ERIC Clearinghouse, 1980). Except for the Latino In-Service Training and Orientation (LISTO) project, however, none of these projects appears to address the bilingual hearing impaired per se.

One of the most comprehensive publications related to bilingual special education in general is the *Bilingual Special Education Resource Guide*, by C. H. Thomas and J. L. Thomas (Phoenix: Oryx Press, 1982). The guide is organized in two parts, one dealing with diverse aspects of the bilingual special education student, e.g., issues and concerns, assessments, curricula, social and emotional needs, parents, career opportunities, and teacher education. The second part covers sources of information: funding agencies, helping agencies, projects, centers, institutes, databases, and specialists.

Oryx Press (2214 N. Central, Phoenix, AZ 85004) has kindly granted permission to select freely from the guide in filling out the following sections here: Information Sources, Funding Agencies, and Journals and Newsletters. The other information here was compiled by the editor.

GILBERT L. DELGADO

I. Information Sources

Alexander Graham Bell Association for the Deaf
3417 Volta Place NW
Washington, DC 20007
(202) 337-5220

Provides information to parents, teachers, and professionals about deafness. Promotes aural/oral approaches for teaching deaf children. Publishes a monthly journal.

Center for Assessment and Demographic Studies
Gallaudet College
800 Florida Avenue NE
Washington, DC 20002
(202) 651-5300

Conducts annual national surveys of deaf students and other research related to the hearing-impaired population. Holdings include very comprehensive demographic data on all hearing-impaired children in the United States.

Clearinghouse on the Handicapped
Office of Special Education and Rehabilitative Services
Switzer Building, Room 3106
Washington, DC 20202
(202) 245-0628

Provides information on services and programs. Offers a free 400-page directory of concerned national organizations.

Closer Look
1201 16th Street NW, Suite 606E
Washington, DC 20036
(202) 822-7900

Disseminates information for parents, teachers, and professionals working with handicapped children. Publishes journals and other materials that parents in particular find helpful.

Conference of Educational Administrators Serving the Deaf
814 Thayer Avenue
Silver Spring, MD 20910
(301) 585-4363

Provides general information about deafness. Publishes a professional journal in cooperation with the Convention of American Instructors of the Deaf.

ERIC Clearinghouse on Handicapped and Gifted Children
Council for Exceptional Children
1920 Association Drive
Reston, VA 22091
(703) 620-3660

Provides abstracting and document reproduction services related to the literature on handicapped children, as part of the Educational Resources Information Center (ERIC).

Minority and Handicapped Concerns Committee
Council for Exceptional Children
1920 Association Drive
Reston, VA 22091
(703) 620-3660

Coordinates activities, seminars, publications, and state-of-the-art developments in bilingual special education.

Multicultural Special Education Network (MUSEP)
School of Education, Campus Box 249
University of Colorado
Boulder, CO 80309
(303) 492-5416

Offers cooperative training and technical assistance to network of constituents. Conducts needs assessments and literature reviews, evaluates activities, and publishes a quarterly newsletter.

National Academy
Gallaudet College
800 Florida Avenue NE
Washington, DC 20002
(202) 651-5480

Provides workshops and training to professionals and the general public, especially concerning delivery of services to deaf people. Offers special training for deaf people in leadership development, the political process, etc.

National Association for Bilingual Education
1201 16th Street NW, Room 405
Washington, DC 20036
(202) 822-7870

Conducts annual national conference on bilingual education and serves as the largest professional association in this field. Publishes a journal (three times a year) and a newsletter (five times a year).

National Association of the Deaf
814 Thayer Avenue
Silver Spring, MD 20910
(301) 587-1788

Offers printed material on deafness. Is a proactive agency of and for deaf people. Has monthly publication and state chapters.

National Center for Law and the Deaf
Gallaudet College
800 Florida Avenue NE
Washington, DC 20002
(202) 651-5454

Disseminates information on legal questions regarding deaf people. Advocates rights of the hearing impaired in litigation involving education, employment, etc. Wrote *Legal Rights of Hearing-Impaired People* (Washington, D.C.: Gallaudet College Press, 1984).

National Clearinghouse for Bilingual Education
1555 Wilson Boulevard, Suite 605
Roslyn, VA 22209
(703) 522-0710

Provides information, newsletters, bibliographies, selected articles, research data, and product and material lists. Has staff assigned to special education. Toll-free hotline: (800) 336-4560, 8:30 a.m. to 5:00 p.m.

National Information Center on Deafness
Gallaudet College
800 Florida Avenue NE
Washington, DC 20002
(202) 651-5109

Responds to inquiries from parents, students, researchers, and others regarding hearing impairment. Provides printed materials on deafness-related topics free or for minimal cost. Houses a splendid orientation exhibit about what deafness is and is not.

II. Bilingual Education Support Service Centers

Supported by the Office of Bilingual Education and Minority
Languages Affairs, U.S. Department of Education

**Bilingual Education
Multifunctional Support
Center**
345 Blackstone Boulevard
The Potter Building
Providence, RI 02906
(401) 274-9548
Adeline Becker

Service Area I
Connecticut, Maine,
Massachusetts, New Hamp-
shire, Rhode Island, &
Vermont

Hunter College of CUNY
695 Park Avenue
New York, NY 10021
(212) 772-4765
Jose Vazquez, Ph.D.

Service Area II
New York

Georgetown University
D.C. Transit Building,
Suite 378
3520 Prospect Street NW
Washington, DC 20007
(202) 625-3540
Ramon Santiago, Ph.D.

Service Area III
D.C., Delaware, Maryland,
New Jersey, North Carolina,
Ohio, Pennsylvania, Virginia,
& West Virginia

**Florida International
University**
School of Education
Tamiami Campus
Miami, FL 33199
(305) 554-2768
Rosa Inclan, Ph.D.

Service Area IV
Alabama, Florida, Georgia,
Kentucky, Mississippi, South
Carolina, & Tennessee

**Community Consolidated
S.D. #15**
Northwest Educational
Cooperative
500 South Dwyer Avenue
Arlington Heights, Il 60005
(312) 870-4106
Minerva Coyne, Ph.D.

Service Area V
Illinois, Indiana, Iowa,
Michigan, Missouri, Min-
nesota, North Dakota, South
Dakota, & Wisconsin

Texas A & I University
Campus Box 152
Kingsville, TX 78363
(512) 595-3788
Maria Barrera, Ph.D.

Service Area VI
Texas; Education Service
Center for Regions I, IV, XX

**Bilingual Education
Multifunctional Support
Center**
University of Texas at El Paso
El Paso, TX 79968
(915) 747-5572
Ernest Perez, Ph.D.

Service Area VII
Arkansas, Louisiana,
Oklahoma, & Texas; Educa-
tion Service Center for Regions
V, XIX

**BUENO Center for
Multicultural Education**
University of Colorado
School of Education
Boulder, CO 80309
(303) 492-5416
Leonard Baca, Ph.D.

Service Area VIII
Colorado, Kansas, Nebraska,
New Mexico, & Utah

Interface Consultants, Inc.
4600 S.W. Kelly
Portland, OR 97201
(503) 222-3065
Francisco Garcia

Service Area IX
Alaska, Idaho, Montana,
Oregon, Washington, &
Wyoming

California State University
5151 State University Drive
Los Angeles, CA 90032
(213) 224-3676
Charles F. Leyba, Ph.D.

Service Area XI*
California—counties of Los
Angeles, Santa Barbara, &
Ventura

**Bilingual Education
Multifunctional Support
Center**
National Hispanic University
255 East 14th Street
Oakland, CA 94606
(415) 451-0511
Edward Aguirre, Ph.D.

Service Area XII
Nevada & California—all
counties north of and in-
cluding San Luis Obispo, Kern,
& Inyo

Colegio Universitario
Metropolitano
P.O. Box E
Rio Piedras, PR 00928
(809) 767-9730
Cesar D. Cruz Cabello

Service Area XIII
Commonwealth of Puerto Rico
& Virgin Islands

Hawaii American Samoa
Bilingual Education Support
Center
Office of Instructional Services
595 Pepeekeo Street,
Building H-1
Honolulu, HI 96825
(808) 395-7561
Salu Reid

Service Area XIV
Hawaii & American Samoa

University of Guam
College of Education
UOG Station
Mangilao, GU 96913
Cable: UNIV GUAM
Telex: 721-6275
International Telephone:
671-734-2921
Robert Underwood

Service Area XV
Commonwealth of Northern
Mariana, Guam, & Trust Ter-
ritory of the Pacific Islands

Bilingual Education
Multifunctional Support
Center
Arizona State University
College of Education
Tempe, AZ 85287
(602) 965-5688
Milo Kalectaca

*Service Area XVI**
Alaska, Arizona, California,
Michigan, Minnesota, Mon-
tana, New Mexico, North
Carolina, Oklahoma, South
Dakota, Utah, Washington,
& Wyoming.

* *Service Area X* is not listed because of no official service center at time of publication. *Service Area XVI* is geared to states having more than 5,000 American-Indian
residents.

III. Office of Bilingual Education and Minority Languages Affairs: Evaluation, Dissemination, and Assessment Centers (EDACs)

Lesley College
49 Washington Avenue
Cambridge, MA 02140
Paul Liberty
(617) 492-0505

Designated Service Area: ED Regions I, II, III, & IV (Connecticut, Maine, Massachusetts, New Hampshire, Rhode Island, Vermont, New York, New Jersey, Puerto Rico, Virgin Islands, Delaware, Pennsylvania, Maryland, Virginia, West Virginia, District of Columbia, Alabama, Florida, Georgia, Kentucky, Mississippi, North Carolina, South Carolina, & Tennessee).

Dallas Independent School District
3700 Ross Avenue
Dallas, TX 75204
Juan Solis
(214) 742-5991

Designated Service Area: ED Regions V, VI, VII, & VIII (Illinois, Indiana, Minnesota, Michigan, Ohio, Wisconsin, Iowa, Kansas, Missouri, Nebraska, Arkansas, Louisiana, New Mexico, Oklahoma, Texas, Colorado, Montana, North Dakota, South Dakota, Utah, & Wyoming).

California State University–Los Angeles Foundation
5151 State University Drive
Los Angeles, CA 90032
Charles Leyba
(213) 224-3676

Designated Service Area: ED Regions IX & X (Arizona, California, Hawaii, Nevada, Guam, Trust Territory of the Pacific, American Samoa, Commonwealth of the Northern Mariana Islands, Alaska, Idaho, Oregon, & Washington).

IV. Funding Agencies

Special Education Programs
U. S. Department of Education
400 Maryland Avenue SW
Washington, DC 20202
(Personnel training, higher education, and school grants)

Office of Bilingual Education and Minority Languages Affairs
400 Maryland Avenue SW
Washington, DC 20202
(Training, fellowships, projects such as materials development, deans grants)

Teacher Centers
400 Maryland Avenue SW
Washington, DC 20202
(Mainstreaming, inservice education grants)

V. Journals and Newsletters

dsh Abstracts
American Speech-Language-Hearing Association
10801 Rockville Pike
Rockville, MD 20852
(Quarterly)

American Annals of the Deaf
The Convention of American Instructors of the Deaf &
Conference of Educational Administrators Serving the Deaf
814 Thayer Avenue
Silver Spring, MD 20910
(6 times/year)

Exceptional Children
Council for Exceptional Children
1920 Association Drive
Reston, VA 22091
(8 times/year)

Hispanic Deaf Newsletter
Hearing Impairment Program
Department of Special Education
University of Nebraska–Omaha
Omaha, NE 68122
(Monthly)

Journal of Special Education
Grune & Stratton, Inc.
111 Fifth Avenue
New York, NY 10003
(Quarterly)

Teaching Exceptional Children
Council for Exceptional Children
1920 Association Drive
Reston, VA 22091
(Quarterly)

The Volta Review
Alexander Graham Bell Association for the Deaf
3417 Volta Place NW
Washington, DC 20007
(Monthly)

Index